How to Enter Heaven

by
Adrian Lickorish

*All booklets are published thanks to the
generous support of the members of the
Catholic Truth Society*

CATHOLIC TRUTH SOCIETY
PUBLISHERS TO THE HOLY SEE

Contents

All rights reserved. First published 2014 by The Incorporated Catholic Truth Society, 40-46 Harleyford Road London SE11 5AY Tel: 020 7640 0042 Fax: 020 7640 0046. Copyright © 2014 The Incorporated Catholic Truth Society.

ISBN 978 1 86082 920 8

1. Introduction

To die, to sleep,
To sleep, perchance to dream. Ay, there's the rub,
For in that sleep of death what dreams may come
When we have shuffled off this mortal coil
Must give us pause.

Hamlet: William Shakespeare (1564-1616)

"No, dear heart," spoke a pleasant voice, which seemed familiar to Prince Andrei, "I say that if it were possible to know what there will be after death, none of us would be afraid of death. That's so, dear heart." Another, younger voice interrupted him: "Afraid or not, all the same you can't avoid it." "But you're still afraid ! Eh, you learned people", said a third, manly voice interrupting the two others. "That's why you artillerists are so learned, because you can tote everything along with you, both vodka and grub." And the owner of the manly voice, probably an infantry officer, laughed."But you're still afraid" the first, familiar voice went on. "Afraid of the unknown, that's what."

War and Peace: Leo Tolstoy (1828-1910)

1.1 That death will come

Today a man is, and tomorrow he appeareth not. Full soon shall this be fulfilled in thee; look then to thy soul's salvation. And when a man is out of sight, soon also he passeth out of mind. O the dullness and hardness of the human heart, that dwelleth only upon things present, rather than upon those to come!

The Imitation of Christ: Thomas à Kempis
(1379/80-1471)

We will all die - each and every one of us. There is no escape. There are no exceptions. Even though for many years we avoid illness or injury, or recover from them, the inevitable is only postponed. One day, the doctor's news will not be good. One day, there will be no more evasions.

In considering our death, we are considering a reality. Most of us, most of the time, refrain from thinking about that reality. Hardly surprising: the part we know - the path to death - is fearful. We see too often a course of pain, loneliness, perhaps humiliation, loss of hope, loss of independence. For many, perhaps most, it will entail a recognition: I did not become the person I wished to be; did not achieve or experience the things I hoped for.

Reflecting on this path brings little joy. When the call comes, when the whistle blows and I clamber up the ladder and go over the top, will my passing be marked with pain, bitterness and regret?

Then, beyond: the unknown. Might the miseries which precede death continue afterwards? Or do we face mere extinction? We hear nothing from family and friends who have gone before: apparently, silence reigns.

So, little wonder that our instinct is to flinch, to turn away, to refrain from investigation and reflection.

Nevertheless, nevertheless: that reaction, almost instinctive, is absurd, an evident nonsense if we pause and think. Facing an inevitable experience, one which might be followed by great good or great ill, we are nitwits if we decline to investigate. What happens? Can I influence my fate? How?

The burden of this booklet is that we can know all we need about the moment of death, and what happens thereafter. We can determine our destination after death by our choices in life. We can have a justified confidence in a joyful destiny after death. Understanding that destiny and developing that confidence will transform our understanding of our life, our death and our future.

The booklet explains the decision we will have to make to attain that joyful destiny, and how to prepare ourselves to make it.

1.2 Carving out time: Priorities

But what were once my assets I now through Jesus Christ count as losses. Yes, I will go further; because of the supreme advantage of knowing Christ Jesus my Lord, I count everything else as loss. For him I have accepted the loss of all other things, and look on them all as filth if only I can gain Christ and be given a place in him...

(*Ph* 3:7-11)

We lead busy lives. Each day we face the urgent, the difficult, sometimes the interesting, sometimes the important. Matters demand our attention, one after another: work, travel, family, friends and acquaintances, all the administrative burdens of modern life, the interruptions, the time spent on communications.

It is all too easy to see the waves and miss the tide.

Yet many of us, perhaps most (even all?) of us, experience - on odd, often unsought occasions - moments of enlightenment. We seem to see with extraordinary clarity, we detect some coherent order, plan, love, in the universe.

Then normal life returns. The recollection of that extraordinary understanding grows dim. The urgent drowns out the important. Year succeeds year, and we press on with daily life. We reflect but little on daunting fundamentals about our purpose and destiny.

Our ultimate fate is a subject hard and uncertain, and may well appear a depressing and unwelcome one. And so the prompting of these moments of enlightenment, the prompting also of logic and reason - we all know we will meet our end in this world, we all know the issue exists - is so often ignored. We know that philosophers and theologians have thought and written extensively about these issues - yet we are reluctant to make the effort to read and reflect.

Those prompts and that knowledge rarely depart fully from us. As in the folk tale, the wolf's distant howl in the forest serves as a reminder of realities we prefer to ignore. There is an uncomfortable concern on the edge of thought. But most of us, most of the time, seek to put it aside.

Perhaps part of the problem is terminology. Theology uses very precise terms, honed over centuries by some of the world's finest minds. They are not always immediately comprehensible to most of us. The subject is also an apt area for metaphor and historic allusion; again, many expressions appear distant or are readily misunderstood in a different era.

It may assist clear thought about the subject of this booklet to set out the starting point simply and without theological terminology:

- IF we retain some consciousness after bodily death; and
- IF that consciousness lasts long (even forever); and
- IF that consciousness can take different forms, some full of joy, some full of pain; and
- IF we can influence those forms by our life –

THEN the issue of our destiny after our death on earth is enormously important. Indeed, if the consciousness lasts long, and the pain or joy is extreme, it is the fundamental issue in our lives. Self-interest demands that we think and act upon it. There is no time to delay: who can know when death will come?

To refrain from investigation and action is to say one has an absolute assurance that these concepts (longevity of consciousness after bodily death and its joy or pain, and our ability to choose our experience) are misconceived.

Yet how can we be certain when we know so little? In any other matter in our life which might have fundamental consequences for us, and which we might be able to determine for our great good or ill, we would focus sustained effort and attention. So should we here.

1.3 Facts, knowledge and an open mind

At work here is that powerful WYSIATI [What You See Is All There Is] rule. You cannot help dealing with the limited information you have as if it were all there is to know. You build the best possible story from the information available to you, and if it is a good story, you believe it. Paradoxically, it is easier to construct a coherent story when you know little, when there are fewer pieces to fit into the puzzle.

Thinking, Fast and Slow: Daniel Kahneman

Imagine a rectangle drawn on paper, the long edges at top and bottom. Inside the rectangle, scattered at random over the enclosed area, are many, many dots. The rectangle itself is divided - like slicing a loaf - by four vertical lines, so forming five slices or sections.

Further imagine that the dots represent all facts and information whatsoever, and the five sections categories of human knowledge.

The left hand section consists of facts and information beyond the capacity of the human mind. We cannot know whether such material exists, or what it is. So the very existence of this category is a speculation. There may or may not be such information. We do not, and will never, know.

The next section represents facts the human mind could know, but which no one yet knows. All scientific knowledge will have been, at one time, in this category.

The third section represents facts which are known to some humans - but not to you. Some languages, advanced science - and much more - falls here.

The fourth represents facts you once knew, but have now (temporarily or permanently) forgotten.

The fifth segment represents your accessible, personal knowledge.

We all, as it were, see only the fifth segment at the outset. To be aware of more - even of the possibility of more - requires effort. There is much of interest and relevance we could all (with application) learn. There is also much we will never learn.

In considering profound subjects like death, judgement, heaven and hell, we need to be cautious. There is much, as it were, to the left of us, hidden from our initial view. It is sensible to recognise that:

- It is worth making some effort to see what others know, which is unknown or inaccessible to us;

- It is sensible to accept that there is likely to be some information, unknown today, which (some) humans will one day learn;

- It is worth bearing in mind that there could well be relevant material beyond human understanding.

So - this is a prompt to humility, and a prompt to an open mind. Are we proceeding on the basis of our knowledge alone? Have we accepted the possible relevance of facts inaccessible to us? Have we attempted to understand what has been discovered or suggested by others? Or is our initial view merely a reflection of the culture and attitudes around us, with some occasional gloss from personal experience? Have we taken into account that there may be relevant information which no one knows?

Do we know, can we express clearly, what we think? Do we know why - upon what information and deductions that conclusion rests? It is worthwhile to pause and consider the foundations for our initial view.

1.4 Duties: to understand, to share, to focus

Jesus came up and spoke to them. He said,"All authority in
Heaven and on earth has been given to me. Go, therefore,
make disciples of all nations; baptise them in the name of
the Father and of the Son and of the Holy Spirit, and teach
them to observe all the commands I gave you. And look, I
am with you always; yes, to the end of time."

(*Mt* 28:19-20)

Rule XXXV: Remember that you are a Christian, and
be neither ashamed nor afraid to speak and act like one
upon all occasions. "Be ready to give an answer to every
man that asketh you a reason of the hope that is in you,"
(*1 P* 3:15); neither affecting to be thought a saint, nor
dreading to be deemed a hypocrite, by any man for
so doing.

Some Rules for the Conduct of Life to which are Added
A Few Cautions for the use of such Freemen of London
as take Apprentices

You don't have to be clever to get to heaven.

Intellectual dexterity, the pleasures of ratiocination,
cut no ice at the pearly gates. Again and again, the figures
criticised in the New Testament are the Pharisees and
lawyers - the clever, the successful, the prominent. And
we can readily see why. These were, of course, people
of great ability and (some at least) of real virtues. Many

fasted, gave to the poor, prayed, exercised self discipline, attended the Temple, lived lives conforming in many ways to the commandments and rabbinical teaching.

But overshadowing these genuine virtues was, too often, pride, and an elevated sense of self and self-will. Too often, these people readily saw themselves as an elite: they knew more; they behaved better, so their will, their views and judgements, should prevail. A dangerous outlook; one we can all recognize as a peril today.

This is not to encourage the opposite extreme, to applaud the deliberate pose of the "Know Nothing". A willing ignorance or disdain of important matters is culpable - like the man who buried his talent, we deserve punishment for a refusal to try. Even a real faith, if ill-informed, resting on emotion, habit and recitation of dogma, is a vulnerable thing. A sudden wave, a serious shock, a facile challenge, may upset the apple cart. Experience shows - and the Church teaches - that our faith should be buttressed by understanding. So far as our ability permits and our circumstances allow, we should make an effort. It is not enough to listen; so far as we can, we should think.

The courteous missionary

We should also share our understanding effectively. If we are convinced of the reality (even the possibility) of heaven (and hell), how can we fail to inform our neighbours - and do so in such a way that they can benefit from our message? How would we react were we to discover, upon our own particular judgement, that our neighbour would have reached heaven if only we had spoken out?

There are, of course, many ways of speaking effectively. My own experience in my career was that many who practised no faith had nevertheless a considerable interest in the spiritual. They had some view that there was, or might be, something in the spiritual realm, that prayer might indeed be effective, that some form of life after death might be a reality. They need and should be presented with an explanation - clear, courteous, and convinced. We need to be prepared to confront opposition, and explain the reality of heaven and hell.

Essential elements of Christianity include the existence of God, the resurrection of Christ, and the reality of heaven and hell. A fundamental role (the fundamental role?) for the Church, formed by the Holy Spirit of God, is to gather humanity to divine life in heaven. We should have the will to explain and debate spiritual issues. We have not lost, and must not give the appearance of having lost, confidence and full belief. We have not come down to regarding classic doctrines as no more than metaphors for ideas now more fully developed by science and sociology. That is not our position. We should make it clear.

We need to speak effectively about the reality we understand, and how to enter heaven.

2. From Where We Stand: Authority and Speculation

2.1 The view from here

Then Peter addressed them, "I now really understand", he said, "that God has no favourites, but that anybody of any nationality who fears him and does what is right is acceptable to him".

(*Ac* 10: 34-35)

"I know myself how little control we have over our sympathies and antipathies," thought Prince Andrei.

War and Peace: Leo Tolstoy (1828-1910)

We all see the world from where we stand. We describe it in our own words, formed by our own minds.

Our perception of truth may be partial - we see only one face of the mountain. It may be limited - our skill with words and theories is imperfect. It may be flawed - for the tools we have, of human mind and thought, are not necessarily the most apt for describing and analysing these matters. Above all, experience shows all too clearly that our techniques of thinking are often fallible. We tend to explain something new by reference to something familiar, to value our own experience too highly, to overweight the vivid, the recent, the small sample, that which accords with current culture or mood.

Those acknowledgements prompt me to say a little about my own starting point. The booklet may be more comprehensible, and helpful, if read in that light. No doubt, like Mr Dick in *David Copperfield*, I have my own versions of King Charles's Troubles, which elbow their way into the text willy nilly, or have a gravitational pull on my speculation or interpretations.

I was baptised in a Roman Catholic ceremony, on a cold winter day in London, in my early infancy. Apparently my Scottish Presbyterian grandmother looked on, tutting at the risk of exposure to a frail infant! I have remained a practising Roman Catholic all my life. I attend Mass every week, and on days of obligation. I go to Confession.

But many of those I have been closest to, those I much admired, have not been Catholics, some not Christians. My mother was an Anglican, as is my wife. Some friends and colleagues belonged to independent Protestant churches. Others again were Jewish, and still others agnostic or simply not able to find it in their heart and mind to believe. In my career in the City of London, I worked with people of a very wide range of nationalities, backgrounds, interests, beliefs.

That experience has profound effects. While I find my Christian faith, and my Catholic denomination, very satisfying, I recoil from the proposition that these are the only way to heaven, not least because so many of these others I have known look far ahead of me in Christ-like qualities, such as practical kindness and unselfishness.

I have seen prayer answered; I have seen what I regard as miracles.

My legal career particularly disposes me to look critically at propositions, to expect reasoned argument and clear definitions. It inclines me to look for an argument developing from principle, through evidence, to example.

Logic and coherence

In retirement from my City career, I could not but be aware that much more of my life on earth was spent than remained. I sought to be clear in my own mind about the four last things - death, judgement, heaven and hell. While I could appreciate the value of assertion, metaphor and dogma in their place, I needed something additional. This was to fit together, logically and in a manner which reflected my own experiences, the overriding principles declared by, and the particular insights of, the Church, the words of the Bible and the expressions of religious writers who had particularly influenced me.

I could contentedly accept a coherent argument which was subject to an overriding caveat - that we are reflecting on things to some extent beyond our reach. I could also freely acknowledge my limits of intellect and knowledge - I was not in the same league as any great minds. So others might well improve or amend my ideas. But I did need something which appeared to me coherent and consistent, was based on established truth and revelation, and could rest comfortably in my heart and mind.

For me, the intellectual journey to an understanding of these issues started with considering established doctrines; the words of the Bible, and those of Christian saints and authors. It continued through reflection on the consistency of specific ideas with revelations about the character of God. I was influenced also by my own experiences, by what I had seen and particularly by people I had come to know and work with, their ideas, conduct and lives. I then sought to summarise the result, so far as possible, in clear and accessible language. This booklet represents the outworking of that journey. I hope others may find it useful for their own passage to understanding, and to assist their entry into, heaven.

2.2 Authority and speculation

Thanks to the assistance of the Holy Spirit, the understanding of both the realities and the words of the heritage of faith is able to grow in the life of the Church:

- through the contemplation and study of believers who ponder these things in their hearts; it is particularly theological research [which] deepens knowledge of revealed truth,

- from the intimate sense of spiritual realities which [believers] experience, the sacred Scriptures grow with the one who reads them,

- from the preaching of those who have received, along with their right of succession in the episcopate, the sure charism of truth.

(*Catechism of the Catholic Church,* para 94)

I do not want to go off the rails. I do not want to disagree with established Christian (and Catholic) doctrine, with those things the Church has formally adopted and taught; but there is a "but".

The Church (very sensibly) proceeds with caution, and does not comment on everything. It has, for example, laid down that we face a "particular judgement" immediately upon death; but it has not laid down the detail of how that works. It has laid down that we have a form of consciousness ("life") after death, but not all the detail of what that involves. It has laid down the importance of sin, virtue, faith, in our hope for heaven; but has not laid down every detail of exactly how those operate in relation to our judgement. So there is a considerable area remaining for proper, reasoned and courteous speculation, made consistently with general principles, the words of the Bible and Church teaching.

The virtues of speculation

There are (at least) three grounds to allow - and indeed encourage - such speculation.

- First, it encourages the development of understanding. The original speculation, the subsequent challenge, the resultant re-working - this is an important process in developing our understanding.

- Second, speculation is part of the adaptation of well-established truths to the particular doubts or concerns of each different age and culture. Current speculation speaks vividly (or can do) to current listeners, in explaining the reasons for established truths.

- Third, speculation can assist the assimilation of great truths by "joining up the dots", by suggesting the pattern and consistency between different, separate truths. Thereby the truths themselves are more readily grasped and adopted.

A fundamental of Jesus's teaching is that what matters is what is in our heart - our fundamental being. So we need to find an explanation which can rest easy there. It is no good repeating dogma we do not believe or do not understand. That is no house built on rock. It is important that we have worked through the issue; got close to it, wrestled with it, and finally arrived at something we can fully believe.

Of course this is not "Liberty Hall". The danger of error is great, so we should be guided by the Church. But the result and expression is not worth tuppence if it fails to reside firmly and comfortably in our heart.

The Church both develops its thinking as time goes on, and expects to speak to each age and culture in terms convincing to its audience. Speculation can assist. Over the last century, there has (for example) been a continuing reflection, and a development of thought on, salvation outside the Church. This has affected views on unbaptised infants (the move away from the doctrine of limbo) and the position of those in other denominations or faiths, or outside all faiths. This is an important ongoing area of reflection and research.

The moment of death

So, a caveat. The idea of a final decision at the moment of death is one I find credible and satisfying. It was popularised by Fr. L. Boros. It can properly be regarded as a speculation. Linked to that is the concept that our ultimate destination reflects our own choice. Again, I find this credible and satisfying. I find Biblical support for it and, above all, support from the revealed nature and purpose of God. Exactly what happens in the process of Christ's "Judgement" of us, how far my analogy of the role of a judge in a jury trial is a helpful one, is an open issue. I very much hope that one function of this booklet will be to prompt reflection among its readers. That may well lead us all further forward.

3. Differences and Difficulties

Langland: And as I sat in this sorrow,
I saw how Nature passed
And Death drew nigh me, and I quaked for dread,
And I called out to Nature, to bring me out of care.
"Look! Old Age, the hoary one is hot on my tracks!
Help and avenge me! Would I were hence!"
Old Age: "If you hope for help, you must hasten into Unity;
Hold you there for ever, until I send for you;
And try to learn some trade there, before you travel thence".
Langland: "O Nature, let me know", said I, "What trade is best to learn?"
Nature: "Learn to love," said Nature, "and leave all other learning".

(*Visions From Piers Plowman*: William Langland
(c. 1332-1386), translated by Nevill Coghill)

3.1 Many different views

In the unity of the love of God, the hearts of Christians are reunited, and this unity is heaven. How beautiful!
St John Vianney, the curé d'Ars (1786-1859)

From opposite standpoints in the Christian world, from different quarters of human life and character, through various expressions of their common faith and hope, through diverse modes of conversion, through different portions of the Holy Scripture will the weary travellers enter the heavenly city and meet each other - "not without surprise"- on the shores of the same river of life.

Dwight L. Moody (1837-1899):
Quoted in *Heaven* by Randy Alcorn

A problem for all - believers of different faiths, members of different denominations, agnostics and atheists: why do we differ? If something is true and important, why do we not share a common understanding?

Since this booklet deals with fundamentals, and will collide with some opinions or preferences, the problem is worth comment.

In Western Europe, the proposition might be put forward that the decline in religious practice shows that, at least in the most advanced countries in the world, there is indeed a coming together of understanding, and it is to an atheist position - there is no God, no heaven, no hell.

There are problems with that picture of an unfolding, shared understanding of the atheist view. First, taking the world as a whole, Western Europe appears atypical: globally, the practice of religion (including Christianity) is increasing, not declining. Second, regarding Western Europe as the "most civilised" or "most advanced" may seem natural if you live here, but recent history and statistics give little support. In terms of economic activity, as well as in terms of issues such as cohesive family groups; care for the elderly; mental health; social cooperation and individual fulfilment; and in our history over the last hundred years, with its wars and persecutions, Western Europe does not score particularly well. If we discard the notion that the world (or the most civilised parts of it) is advancing steadily to an agreed atheist position, the problem remains. We do not share a common view. Christians disagree among themselves on some matters; Christians disagree with other faiths; and all faiths disagree with agnostics and atheists. Why so?

Responses to difficulties

There are two familiar, but misplaced, responses to the problem of different understandings; and four others which, to the author at least, carry conviction.

The two misplaced responses are:

- Those holding the other view (whatever that is) are malign or stupid; or
- The existence of conflicting views justifies the agnostic position - I simply do not, and cannot, know.

As to the first response (our opponents are foolish, or malignant, or both), personal experience gives it the lie. Most of us (probably all of us) have met some good people who were practising Christians, and some good people who were not. We have met highly intelligent people who were practising Christians, and highly intelligent people who were not. And we have met good and inspiring people of different denominations and faiths, and some of no religious conviction at all.

The second response (the agnostic position) may at first sight appear attractive. Perhaps it is the reasonable, the open-minded, the mature and generous reaction, to a difficult and uncertain issue?

Deeper reflection shows its weaknesses, and very real dangers.

What is an agnostic?

The first weakness is of definition. The term is too broad. "Agnostic" conceals the very many, very different thoughts and approaches that crowd the space between certainty of belief, and certainty of non-belief. "There might be a God, and life after death"; "There could be life after death"; "I think there is something there in spiritual terms, beyond the physical world"; "I cannot believe in complete extinction"; "I think there is probably no life after death, but cannot be sure"; "I would be inclined to believe, but find it difficult in the face of the evil and suffering in the world"; "Sometimes I think there is some reality in a spiritual world, sometimes not"- and so on. Each is a very different position. Each needs to be considered individually, and the issues relevant to each position considered carefully. Each is likely to call forth different conduct in life, and a different degree and area of further, ongoing reflection and investigation. What would be relevant and important to one person at one place on this spectrum would not be to another.

A broad, single category blunts the process of investigation and reflection. It closes the mind. In effect, it says:

- "Because I am not sure of everything in this area, I cannot hold any view"
- "Because I am less than certain, I cannot act at all on a conjecture, a perceived possibility, a realistic chance, even a likelihood".

That cannot be right. In no other area would we accept such a negative, passive position. We know well, in everyday life, that if something has important consequences for us, we (may) think about it, research it, consider it. But we also know well that we frequently have to act on less than a certainty. It is a practical necessity; it may embrace a matter very important to us; and it often turns out well.

The second weakness is that the response ignores an asymmetry of benefit and loss in the issue.

The consequences of belief, if belief is true, are potentially immeasurably wonderful. The consequences of wilful lack of belief, if belief is true, are potentially terrible.

But the reverse in each case has quite different - and far lesser - consequences. If we believe and are wrong, the consequences are insignificant. If we disbelieve and are correct, we never even know. This asymmetry of consequences - Pascal's Wager - is commented on further below.

The danger of the agnostic position is that it hides from us a reality of choice. If heaven exists, every thought, word or deed of ours may have a relevance to our destination. Each of those may make it more, or less, likely that we will reach heaven. In that light, we will (or should) be aware of the consequences for our ultimate destination of a train of thought, conversation or action.

If heaven does not exist, we can dispense with that reflection.

We need to be clear on which route we are following. To think that there may be some form of afterlife with (at the least) pleasant or unpleasant experiences, and that our destination is in some way determined by our character (which influences and is influenced by our conduct) during our earthly existence, but to make no effort to reflect and to shape our belief and conduct, is madness.

The danger of agnosticism is the encouragement, in practice, to ignore the possible impact of belief and conduct on destination. It encourages us to behave, in practice, as if our belief was a convinced atheism - a wholly different position.

3.2 A Suggestion: freedom and growth

Yet even if Revelation is already complete, it has not been made completely explicit; it remains for Christian faith gradually to grasp its full significance over the course of the centuries.

(Catechism of the Catholic Church, para 66)

There are four responses to the problem of our different understandings of life after death, God, heaven and hell which carry conviction. These are:

- Inevitability;
- Humility;
- Growth;
- Good.

These responses accord with a Christian understanding. The terminology maybe unusual for non-Christians; but I believe most people can find elements in their experience consistent with these responses.

Inevitability

We have the extraordinary gift of freedom. We may choose to believe or not. Neither our minds, nor the conditions of the world, compel us to belief. There are many experiences and circumstances which point us to God. Some, as they occur, possess enormous power and clarity. But, even here, because we are weak, we forget; we excuse; we fall back;

we seek the comfortable ahead of the true. Thus we are never in the position, in the long run, where the assistance to understanding given by God's grace overwhelms our freedom to choose.

Then there is Satan. Malign, powerful, ever seeking our destruction, the devil finds opportunity in our uncertainty. Satan and his legions will always question faith, stimulate uncertainty, delay reform, blur vision, encourage the thoughts and conduct which will destroy us.

To those outside a traditional faith, the concept of Satan may at first appear archaic. But consider: have you not experienced personally, seen in others, something which looks and feels like a directed, intelligent, persistent, force of and temptation to evil? The character of Satan is not an expression of creativity. It is a reflective response to the reality of human life, experienced over centuries (indeed, millennia). The Catholic understanding (broadly shared with many other denominations and faiths) is that there are many beings that are not visible but exert physical effects in the world. Among these, some have intellect and will (angels) and some of these are malign (demons). The effects of the malign ones can be seen most clearly in consistent strategies to bring about diabolical goals, in the lives of both individuals and nations.

These factors, freedom and Satan and his legions, will prompt many to hold different views.

Humility

God is eternal, omniscient, omnipotent, all good. We are not.

We do not have the character or mental ability to comprehend him, his plans or works, beyond that which is sufficient for our salvation. We will never fully do so.

Each of us is different, each deliberately created to be unique. It must follow that each of us has the capacity for some particular insight into God and his purposes more clearly or more extensively than others. We are all looking at the mountain, but at different parts, with different eyes, from different angles. The other person's view, different from ours, may still be accurate, in whole or part. It may well have something to teach us, not necessarily to correct our own view, but to add to it.

Not every vision will be of equal scope. One view may describe a huge col; another a single stone. But the accurate description of even one stone has value. It adds to our knowledge and understanding of the true picture. We need to remind ourselves: every single person has the capacity to see one particular aspect of God and his purposes with unique clarity or insight: a valuable caution.

Growth

From our earliest recorded history, the Holy Spirit has operated to lead mankind to an understanding of God. That understanding has grown through mystics, prophets and philosophers, evidenced by practice and writing.

The Holy Spirit could speak to Persians, Egyptians, and Greeks. Above all, the people of Israel had a unique role in responding to the truths revealed and, increasingly, understood by its prophets and people.

Jesus not only makes possible our salvation, He also explains fundamental truths, and facilitates the understanding we need for salvation. With Jesus, revelation is complete. But it is not completely explicit. Throughout the Church's history, the faithful have pondered his words; we need to continue to do so. We need to read the Bible. All of us need assistance from others in understanding it. The great commentators - be they St Augustine or St Thomas Aquinas - still speak eloquently to us. But theirs is not the last word. Further commentators will add to (and may correct, or re-emphasise, or re-focus) their words. It would be a poor state indeed if Christians had no more guidance now than when my village church was built in 1080.

That is not to say that some of the best and wisest individuals did not live 100 or 1000 or 1900 years ago (clearly, they did). It is not to suggest that someone living long ago may not have enjoyed extraordinary insight into, and love of, God (clearly, many did). Their writings teach us much. Indeed, we cannot pretend to match the Apostles. But it is to suggest that we should have developed some additional insights, explanations and examples to communicate a clear understanding of the words of Jesus (and the words of the Bible). It is to suggest that there should be an ongoing development of the ability to explain eternal truths in a manner apt for each new culture and society. It is to suggest that truths may become stale, or forgotten or overlooked or lose their power or priority as cultures change, and will need new expressions, revival.

Good

We aim for a shared understanding of the truth. On the way, differences seem inevitable. Where those differences lead to the loss of love of neighbour (as they frequently do) they are a source of evil. But not all the consequences of these differences of view are evil. Here, as elsewhere, in the end all things work for good. The expression of different views prompts study and reflection. It has often reawakened or re-emphasised ideas which have become ignored, or underrated or taken for granted. John Bunyan's uplifting, inspiring tale of *The Pilgrim's Progress*, the first part of which was published in 1678, is the work of a Puritan, a Dissenter, in Kipling's words:

> A tinker out of Bedford,
> A vagrant oft in quod,
> A private under Fairfax,
> A minister of God.

But Bunyan's theme of the pilgrimage of the Christian, its dangers, temptations and uncertainties, is a magnificent expression of a similar theme used by Walter Hilton, a canon of the Augustinian Order at the priory of St Peter, in Thurgarton, near Nottingham. Walter Hilton lived from 1330 - 1395/6, and wrote in *The Scale of Perfection* (Chapter 21) of the pilgrimage of faith, the journey to Jerusalem, and the perils and temptations on the way.

Here is an instance of authors of different denominations, apparently very different experiences of life and in different eras, nevertheless seizing on, and developing, the same telling metaphor for spiritual development.

Reflection on the revelation of the three divine persons of the one God, Father, Son and Holy Spirit, who are revealed in Scripture and who are known together as the Trinity, may prompt a useful insight here. The Trinity consists of three distinct, unlimited persons with distinct roles, sharing one substance, one nature of God. Perhaps a reminder that difference can reinforce one truth; that uniformity is not a sure guide to strength and fulness. Of course, the analogy cannot be pressed too far. The persons of the Trinity do not disagree. But a reminder, nonetheless, that several distinct strands may make a stronger rope. There are uses in difference.

Different denominations may have different areas of truth to emphasise. That can be a strength, like different regiments, with different traditions and expertise, in one army. Different faiths may also add to a growing understanding. The words (and practices) of faiths outside Christianity may have a freshness to a Christian, and a startling coincidence with Christian doctrine, which can open hearts and minds. Equally, differences may emphasise some unique and important elements of Christianity, otherwise too easily taken for granted.

Even the views and campaigns of atheists and agnostics may bear fruit. Their powerful drive to discuss matters of faith, and their energy, all emphasise the importance of fundamental issues of belief. This can be an awakening bugle for many passive Christians. Their arguments prompt Christians to reflect, develop, define. Overall, Christians are stimulated to respond effectively. We are challenged to present our view of fundamental truth in terms and by methods apt for the world and people of our day.

As in every area of life, a degree of challenge prompts the best performance, from all of us.

3.3 Difficulties

...doubt not, but in vallie and in plaine
God is as here , and will be found alike
Present, and of His presence many a signe
Still following thee, still compassing thee round
With goodness and paternal love, His face
Express, and of his steps the track divine.

Paradise Lost: John Milton (1608-1674)

There are a number of concerns frequently expressed about belief in heaven and hell. These need to be articulated, and answered, early in the review of how we enter heaven, or we may never start on the journey.

Set out below are five concerns, with a summary response:

- If God wishes us to come to heaven, why is the path not made clear?

- If God wishes all to come to heaven, why is faith so important? Many will not have any.

- If sin corrupts us, and leads us away from heaven, then why are we so made as to be inclined to sin?

- If we (or most of us) would not invent or create hell, why does God?

- If we (or most of us) would not send anyone - even our most loathed enemies - to an eternal hell, why does an all-good God?

The answer to the first concern is that the path to heaven is indeed straightforward. No intellectual distinction, no perfect life free of sin, is required. Heaven is open (and has been opened by Jesus's sacrifice) to all who would enter in.

The answer to the second concern is that faith, as the beginning of a life of grace, is a sure path - but we need to define what we mean by faith carefully. The path is unlikely to be as narrow as we are sometimes inclined to make it. We need to beware of saying: "faith is what I believe; those who do not believe what I believe have no faith".

The answer to the third concern is that (as we all know from daily life), mind leads body. What we think and what we say instructs what we do; and thoughts and words and deeds shape our character. We have great freedom. We become the person we choose. We can indeed make ourselves into such a person who would choose not to come to heaven.

The answer to the fourth concern is that hell must exist if heaven exists and we retain our freedom. If we are invited to come to heaven and refuse, we must go somewhere else: that is to hell. The characteristics of hell derive entirely from the absence of God; from our character; and from the presence of Satan and his legions.

The answer to the fifth concern is that God condemns no one to hell. Anyone in hell is there as a result of their own choice. Anyone who accepts the grace of God, makes the choice for heaven, reaches heaven.

4. The Possibility of Understanding

Only see: all rational beings, angels and men, have in them, each individually, two principal active faculties, one, a faculty of knowledge, and the second, a faculty of love; and God, their maker, is forever beyond the reach of the first of these, the intellectual faculty; but by means of the second, the loving faculty, He can be fully grasped by each individual being, to such an extent that each single loving soul may, by virtue of love, embrace within itself Him who is fully sufficient (and beyond comparison more than fully) to fill all the souls and angels that can ever exist.

The Cloud of Unknowing, Chapter 4:
Anon, English, about 1370

Our faith is a light, coming to us naturally from Him who is our everlasting day, our Father, and our God. By this light, Christ, our mother, and the Holy Spirit, our good Lord, lead us through these passing years. The light is measured to our individual needs as we face our night.

Revelations of Divine Love, Chapter 83:
Julian of Norwich (c. 1342-1416)

4.1 A vain hope?

I know that you are all powerful;
What you conceive, you can perform.
I was the man who misrepresented your intentions
With my ignorant words...
Before, I knew you only by hearsay
But now, having seen you with my own eyes
I retract what I have said,
And repent in dust and ashes.

(Jb 42:2-3, 5-6)

Is it all too distant?

Is knowledge of God, heaven, hell, judgement, the major tenets of faith, so thoroughly "other", so far separated from our abilities, our experience, our culture, the tools we have to think with, as to be inevitably a useless, fruitless study? Should we leave well alone that which we cannot do properly?

Of course we can never comprehend everything about God. But we can comprehend sufficient for our salvation. Failure to try, a defeatist attitude, exposes us to danger. We are deliberately ignoring understanding which will assist us. The risk of serious error, with serious (perhaps fatal) consequences, lies before us.

Both reasoned, intellectual knowledge about God, and mystical knowledge of God, are possible. The author of *The Cloud of Unknowing* regards mystical experience, gained through love, as a route to a direct understanding of God. Rational thought is another route. It provides an important foundation and has a particular value in being readily accessible and readily communicated.

The material for us to consider comes in many forms: the writings of powerful minds (for example, St Augustine, St Thomas Aquinas, C. S. Lewis); experiences of visionaries and of saints (for example, Julian of Norwich, St Teresa of Avila, George Herbert); fundamentally changed lives (St Augustine, John Newton); the widely reported effect of prayer and meditation.

We have much advice, from many eras and cultures. The author of *The Cloud of Unknowing* sets forth an approach which has echoes in the writings of St John of the Cross (in Spain in the 17th century); Trappist meditation; the Jesus Prayer ("Lord Jesus Christ, have mercy on me", consistently repeated, of the *Philokalia* in the Orthodox tradition). Of course each is distinct and different, but there are also startling overlaps. Very different eras and traditions have powerful common voices: something unexpected, which requires reflection from anyone open minded.

How can we purport to hold a view on these matters without proper examination of an extraordinary quantity of relevant evidence? That evidence says that an understanding of God (and our path to heaven) is attainable. Is it not mere folly to refrain from, at the least, reading (some) of that evidence? In any other area of our lives, such a deliberate spurning of potentially material evidence on an important issue would be regarded as crass, as professional negligence. We should, at least, carry our normal standards of due diligence into this enquiry!

5. Choices and Consequences

Elijah stepped out in front of all the people. "How long",
he said, "do you mean to hobble, first on one leg, then
on the other? If Yahweh is God, follow him; but if Baal,
follow him." But the people had nothing to say.

(1 K: 21-22)

Décider, c'est choisir.

Marshal Ferdinand Foch (1851-1929)

5.1 Six questions

A survey of 2,060 people showed 53 percent believe in life
after death, 55 per cent believe in heaven and 70 per cent
believe in the human soul.

Report of study carried out between October
and November 2008 for the Theos Think Tank

Do you believe in life after death? Do you believe that any
form of consciousness at all does, or may, survive death?
Are you convinced; or believe it likely; or possible; or not
impossible; or do you have some inchoate feeling that
"there might be something in it?

Alternatively, are you certain that there is no such thing,
and certain that you are aware of all the facts - that there
are no "unknown unknowns" which might alter that view?

If there is no form of consciousness after death, there is no foundation upon which to build a vision or understanding of heaven and hell. So thinking about your position on this first question is important.

It sounds a clear question, demanding a clear and immediate answer - yes or no. In fact (as with so many important issues), some sustained thinking is required to provide a convincing opinion, and one that guides us in coming to a view on heaven and hell. Even the phrase "life after death" may blunt thought. It is so familiar.

It carries the burden of metaphors, pictures and assumptions (clouds, harps, long white robes). Above all, it tends to encourage the thought not just of continuity, but of similarity: that "life" after death will be rather like life on earth but in some way cleaned up and pared down - earnest, colourless, "sanitised": a dangerously misleading view.

Accordingly, I use the phrase "consciousness after death" here in an attempt to deter some inaccurate assumptions. The aim is to encourage reflection on whether there is any form of conscious survival of some essence of our character; and to avoid confusing this first issue with the subsequent question, of the nature of our surroundings and powers after bodily death. The second issue, the nature of the experience after bodily death, is commented on below.

There are six stages in the thought process for this first issue - six questions to be considered.

FIRST: Is there, in any form whatever, consciousness after death, or not?

SECOND: If there is, does everyone share the same form of this consciousness, or not?

THIRD: If there are differences, what causes them?

FOURTH: Is it important to form a view on this matter during our lives?

FIFTH: At what point (if any) does some form of belief in consciousness after death lead to belief in God, heaven and hell?

SIXTH: If we are uncertain, are there general factors favouring any particular view?

5.2 Consciousness after death

Never weather-beaten sail more willing bent to shore,
Never tired pilgrim's limbs affected slumber more,
Than my weary spirit now long to fly out of my troubled breast,
O come quickly, sweetest Lord, and take my soul to rest.

Thomas Campion (1567-1620)

I had the feeling that everything had been sloughed away; everything I aimed at or wished for or thought, the whole phantasmagoria of earthly existence, fell away or was stripped from me - an extremely painful process. Nevertheless, something remained; it was as if I now carried along with me everything I had ever experienced or done, everything that had ever happened to me. I might also say; it was with me and I was it. I consisted of my own history and I felt with great certainty: this is what I am.

Memories, Dreams, Reflections:
Dr Carl Jung (1875-1961)

Is there any form of consciousness after death, or not?

The atheist view would say there is not. We face the bleak prospect of extinction. We die, and there is no more. No joy, no pain, no awareness, no change. Not even the satisfaction of knowing our philosophy was right. Nothing at all.

Well, in theory it could be so.

A considered position would rest on a thorough review of the evidence. For the atheist, the conclusion would need to be that there was no evidence to disturb the clear certainty of our extinction on death. The atheist would also need to be sure that all the relevant evidence had been considered.

There are four categories of evidence. These are:

- Holy writing and tradition (the Bible, and also the holy writings of other faiths);

- Visions (experienced by both Christians and those of other faiths);

- "Near Death Experiences" (from individuals revived after clinical death, many in modern times and under modern medical conditions);

- Modern science.

Holy writing and tradition

The writings, traditions and burial practices of many cultures, throughout history, have affirmed a belief in life after death. The detail is expressed in many ways, reflecting the traditions of the relevant culture. There are, interestingly, many fundamental similarities of belief across very different traditions. These cultures envisage an experienced consciousness after death; joy or pain according to worldly conduct (with particular rewards for unselfish conduct - courage, charity, loyalty); a meeting with God (or gods).

A "no consciousness" view has to say that all the people who followed these views are all, entirely, wrong. A bold view.

Are you really brighter than all these people? The author has read C.S. Lewis; received a prize from, and talked to, Lord Denning. He knows very well how far he lags behind them in intellect. There are so many, many others. Consider for a moment: Tertullian, born in Carthage in AD 150, author of numerous works in Latin and Greek; Augustine of Hippo, born in AD 354 in what is now Algeria, a brilliant teacher and writer; Anselm, born in Italy in 1053, who became Archbishop of Canterbury and formulated the ontological argument for the existence of God; Descartes, born in France in 1596, still regarded as one of the world's leading mathematicians; Isaac Newton, born in England in 1642, one of the world's leading scientists; Joseph

Priestley, born in England in 1733, a leading chemist of his era; J.R.R. Tolkien, born in South Africa in 1892, a scholar, a teacher and writer. Are we brighter than them? Even now, do we know more than them, are we able to expound their area more cogently than they did?

Countless people of brilliant intellect through the ages have held the view that life continues after death. Are we really confident that our view is superior to theirs? Unless we are nitwits, we cannot believe that we are cleverer than St Thomas Aquinas. So how can we disdain his views on heaven, formed over years of study and reflection, without at the least reading his explanations? We need to ask ourselves: is any negative response driven by culture, convenience and unwillingness to investigate?

Visions

Another powerful indicator. There have been countless descriptions of heaven and hell, throughout the ages. Many are vouchsafed by well-known figures, people whose honesty is undoubted. Many, judged by their other writings, are people of powerful intellect and good judgement. A very few examples: St Dominic (1170-1221); St Catherine of Siena (1347-1380); St Teresa of Avila (1515-1582); the Blessed Anne Catherine Emmerich (1774-1824); St John Vianney, the Curé of Ars (1786-1859); St John Bosco (1815-1888); Père Lamy (1855-1931); more recently, Sr Lucia in the visions at

Fatima (1917). There are many, many others, up to and including the present day. Such visions are not rare.

There is no doubt that these people honestly believe they have seen and experienced heaven or hell, have seen life after death and the form it takes. It has made a most profound impact upon them. Do we accept that they are indeed reporting what they believe they experienced? Do we accept their interpretation of that experience? Either they are right, or not. If right, a series of dramatic conclusion unfolds. The fact that we find these odd or unattractive is not a good ground for rejecting them.

We may, of course, accept that the report accurately records what they experienced, but argue with the interpretation. Perhaps their experience, though vivid, was the product of internal, uncontrolled, brain activity, caused by some chemical imbalance or fault. We are familiar with nightmares: perhaps these visions are somewhat similar?

That is a possibility, but we do need to be careful here. We should not start with a firm prejudice that there is no consciousness after death, and then refuse to consider the evidence, or assume without analysis that it can be explained away. The better view is to accept that there is, in visions, a form of evidence. It is something we can neither explain nor deny. It is something which, by our own judgement, we cannot finally determine as true or false; but it does exist.

Near death experiences

The extraordinary powers of modern medicine are such that people are, from time to time, resuscitated after clinical death. In many cases, they report their experiences. One example is the quotation above, describing Jung's experience after a heart attack, while unconscious in hospital in Switzerland in July 1944. There are interesting parallels with Christian doctrine, of the painful "stripping away" process (purgatory) and the coming to an understanding of the core of self (the soul), shaped by our whole life.

Many of these experiences are vivid, and speak of a form of consciousness, with a recognition of others, an understanding prompted by impulses akin to our powers of sight, hearing, thinking. Interestingly, some who have reported these experiences had no religious belief beforehand. Others were, before the experience, convinced atheists. An example is the philosopher, A.J. Ayer. A well-known atheist, he was revived after his heart had stopped. He reported various experiences while "dead", and concluded: "My recent experiences have slightly weakened my conviction that my genuine death will be the end of me, though I continue to hope that it will be".

There is no doubt that people have had these experiences. The only issue, as with the visions, is what they mean. Again, one could envisage that they are a mere chemical function in the brain. Perhaps at the moment of death some chemical floods the brain (or is removed from the brain) and this causes the illusion of these experiences.

That is not impossible. It is, however, odd. The experience apparently occurs only at a medical state of or closely approximating to death - not upon any other occasion when our mind and body are undergoing extraordinary events. Further, the elements of the experience do not always coincide with the individual's previous views or recollected knowledge. So, if we were to approach this with an open mind, we would say that, again, these events provide some (not alone conclusive) evidence for some form of consciousness after bodily death. It is not something that can be ignored, or brushed aside without regard.

Science

If faith is true, it should be consistent with (and have nothing to fear from) science, and vice versa. These are two paths up the same mountain, of the full truth about our existence in this universe. They explore reality from different perspectives - sometimes expressed as the How (science) and the Why (religion). Experiences gained from progress in science can also help us think about the challenge of consciousness after death. Three areas are especially relevant:

- Appreciation that the strange, the unexpected, is often true;

- Evidence of change and continuity within our ongoing "self";
- The laws of thermodynamics.

The first point is the important lesson from science that the extraordinary, the unpredicted, the counter-intuitive, is often true. We live in a much stranger, wilder world than most of us think, a world requiring great leaps of creative imagination to understand.

Science and the unexpected

Apparently, I don't sit on a chair. Instead, the negatively charged fields of the chair and my body repel each other - so I sit one angstrom (a hundred millionth of a centimetre) above the chair. Apparently, that piece of sawn 4x4 wood is not solid at all, but mostly empty space. The wood is made up of atoms. Each atom has a central nucleus made up of protons and neutrons. Far beyond that central nucleus, electrons are orbiting. The *volume* of the atom is mostly made up of the space between the central nucleus and the outer, orbiting electrons - but over 99% of its *mass* is made up of the nucleus.

To the non-scientist, strange indeed: a caution, and a reminder, that in our everyday world, the world we think we understand as we go about our daily lives, things are far more complex and unexpected than we assume. So we should not be too confident in saying consciousness after death cannot be true, because our common sense (or our senses generally) do not support the idea. In so many areas, science has already shown our common sense to be a poor guide.

Atoms and the soul

The second scientific analogy is about our bodies. They are made up of billions of tiny atoms. Those atoms have a long life - much, much longer than a human life. Some may last thousands of years, some millions, some billions or as long as the cosmos. Before being part of our bodies, they served as part of all manner of things, including trees, stones, animals, other people. They will do so again. Indeed, as it is more poetically put in Ecclesiastes "The dust returns to the earth from which it came; and the spirit returns to God who gave it" (12:7).

Further "our" atoms will be replaced many times in the course of our life. Yet we see a consistency in our character, from 8 year old to 80 year old. So there is something cohesive and consistent in us, apart from the physical structure of our bodies.

Our essential being - described by faith as our soul - survives the replacement of the physical material, the atoms, of our bodies. It is at the least a credible possibility that the fate of our soul is analogous (although distinct) from that of the atoms of our bodies. Just as "our" atoms continue an existence in a different form after leaving our body, so may our soul.

Is that suggestion, for the soul, any more strange than the proven fate of the atoms of our bodies?

Energy

The third scientific analogy relates to the First Law of Thermodynamics.

This law of physics applies to the conservation of energy. In summary, it states that energy cannot be created or destroyed - only maintained or converted to a different form (for example, from movement to heat).

This law provides an interesting analogy for our soul. Just as wood is not destroyed in a fire but transformed (to heat, light, ash); and as our body is not destroyed in death but transformed (into its constituent atoms), so perhaps with our soul.

Our soul - the essential personality we have shaped by experience, choice, memory, character - is also transformed into the consciousness which survives death. A speculation, of course; but one consistent with a law of physics present in our universe since its creation.

In Summary

Where does this review of sources of evidence take us? At the least, to recognise that:

- There is some evidence for consciousness after death;
- The arguments against consciousness after death are not decisive, and it is dangerously easy to start from an a priori

conviction that "life after death simply cannot be true", from a closed mind, a reluctance to admit a possibility;

- Scientific truth shows us many dramatic examples of reality beyond - and contrary to - what we would be inclined to believe by "common sense".

The reality of ourselves and our world is already proved to be far stranger than we care to admit. We already know that a bet that the strange is not true is likely to be bad.

5.3 The forms of consciousness after death, and causes of difference

He will bring to light everything that is hidden in darkness and reveal the designs of all hearts.

(1 Co 4:5)

What we hear from our friends who have passed over, people who came back to share with us, is that every human being, after this transition, is going to have to face something that looks very much like a television screen. You will be given an opportunity - not to be judged by a judgemental God - but to judge yourself, by having to review every single action, every word and every thought of your life.

On Life After Death:
Elizabeth Kubler-Ross M.D. (1926-2004)

Suppose you think there is, or may be, some form of consciousness after death.

That takes you to a recognition that religious belief is a reasonable response, and may indeed be true; but it is still, at that stage, not the only possible answer. There are other possibilities.

One could envisage, for example, that some law of physics, currently unknown, allows the "imprint" of personality to cohere and survive after bodily death. That "imprint" could include some form of awareness - even if only a limited self-awareness.

Apart from the question of cause, there is the question of nature. Do we all share an identical experience of post-bodily death consciousness, or not? The same evidence for consciousness after death noted above - holy writing and tradition; visions; near death experiences; science - suggest our experiences are not the same, in content or quality.

In addition, there are our own lives - and geometry.

Life choices

We see from our own, everyday experience how the choices we make alter our character, and our character determines our experience of life.

We see some people who are selfish, avaricious, unreliable - perhaps we have had to work with such a person. We see how one deliberately bad choice of theirs leads to another, and character gradually becomes firmly cast. The selfish act becomes part of a pattern of repeated selfish acts; and that becomes a predictable state. The quality of the act has become the quality of the person. The selfish act, repeated, has moulded the man - into the selfish man.

Geometry

The geometric proof is a simple one: two things which equal the same third thing, equal each other. The reverse is also true. Things which are different equal different things, have different properties. We might expect virtuous lives to lead after bodily death to ends appropriate for the souls shaped by such lives. We might expect vicious lives to lead to ends after bodily death appropriate for the souls shaped by such lives. But we would not expect the end after bodily death of a virtuous life, and the end of a vicious life, to be the same or in any way similar. The different lives will have formed clear different souls, different things; and those different things will react differently, have different experiences.

Speculation again - but with logic and analogy to support it. Again and again, the belief systems of societies through the ages have stated that while there is some form of consciousness after death, it is not the same for all. Each person has an individual experience, and the nature of that experience is in some way connected with and directed by the aggregate effect of the choices made in life.

Continuity and experience

So we are led to these possibilities: that in some way our unique character, our "imprint", continues after bodily death; that the continuing "imprint" has some form of awareness; and that the experience of that awareness differs for each of us. The fundamental divide in the nature of that experience is between what we might describe as the bad or selfish soul, and the good or unselfish soul.

5.4 Why form a view in life?

...all would have Christ to be their saviour in the next world, and to help them into heaven when they die, by His power and merits with God. But this is not willing Christ to be your saviour, for His salvation, if it is had must be had in this world; if He saves you, it must be done in this life, by changing and altering all that is within you, by helping you to a new heart, as He helped the blind to see...

The Spirit of Prayer: William Law (1686-1761): quoted in *The Way of the English Mystics:* Gordon L. Miller

In death it becomes possible for us to posit something absolute by way of our decision, i.e to open ourselves up to the absolute. Since, however, a decision like this realizes once and for all the whole extent of man's dynamism, completely transforming it into being, existence with this unhampered decision reaches the state in which all its possibilities of decision in regard to its last end are exhausted, and this is the domain of ultimate finality.

The Moment of Truth: Fr Ladislaus Boros SJ

Why not wait and see? We will find out anyway upon death. We cannot be sure now; so relax, forget it, go with the flow. A common course to steer, often without full consideration - for there are significant perils.

First, if there is a possibility that heaven and hell exist, coming to the right destination is of fundamental importance. So one should act in relation to anything which might affect our destination with great care. This is not an area for careless decisions (or absence of decisions).

Second, mind leads body. What we think determines how we act. If we defer our decision on whether to believe in heaven, we will have no basis for acting, in our life, in the manner suggested by Church and Bible to lead to heaven. That matters, since our conduct in this life alters our fundamental character, our soul, and it is our soul which survives bodily death. The form of our soul at death leads on to the form of experience thereafter.

If we are inclined to a "scientific" view, that some presently unknown law of physics explains consciousness after death, the position is clear (albeit speculative). The form of the soul at death determines the nature of the experiences after death. So we should live a life designed to form our soul in a shape to experience a joyful consciousness after bodily death.

If we are inclined to a religious explanation, if we are inclined to believe in God, the same reasoning applies, but there may be a preliminary question: why no "second chance"?

If God created us, and loves us, and wishes for us to come to heaven, why can we not reform after bodily death, when we fully understand the choices? Would that not be more equitable?

Beyond the moment of death: too late!

Our invitation at the moment of death, to come to God, is a simple one.

We need no further training or experience to respond. We are fully able to accept the invitation to heaven without further ado.

We have had in life all the opportunity we need to form our soul so as to come to God (and heaven). If we die in infancy or very young, we have not been drawn away from him by the exercise of power and selfishness. If we die later, we have seen enough to distinguish clearly between kindness and cruelty, selfish and unselfish behaviour, love and hate.

Our fundamental inclination - for or against God - is fixed at death. Our soul chooses at the moment of death. The choice is fully free. It expresses, entirely truthfully, the nature and desire of the soul. Experiences thereafter, including even the pain and despair of hell, will not change that fundamental character of the soul. If offered the choice again and again, it would still reject heaven, for it would still - like Satan - insist on the priority of self-will (which cannot be accommodated in heaven). The soul will indeed wish for its agony to cease, but never at the cost inevitable in a choice of heaven - giving up all, and accepting the sovereignty of God. No amount of time or opportunity would change the basic inclination: do we wish to come to God?

A soul which assents to God, comes to heaven and to unimaginable joy.

It will (obviously) never choose to depart. A soul which has reached such a shape that, by the moment of death, it chooses self over God has not the material left in it to be reformed. It has a fixed character, and no pains of hell will induce it to change; it cannot.

5.5 Towards God

The moment you say that one set of moral values can be better than another, you are, in fact, measuring them both by a standard, saying that one of them conforms to that standard more nearly than the other ... if your moral ideas can be truer, and those of the Nazis less true, there must be something - some Real Morality - for them to be true about...

If anyone will take the trouble to compare the moral teaching of, say, the ancient Egyptians, Babylonians, Hindus, Chinese, Greeks, and Romans, what will really strike him will be how very like they are to each other and to our own.

Mere Christianity: C.S. Lewis (1898-1963)

We do well to remember the experiences of history. *Mere Christianity* was broadcast (and then published) during the Second World War. The Nazi comment was based on a then current reality. Since 1945 we have seen plenty of other examples of appalling cruelty. Mankind is (and ever has been) capable of hideous things.

Every time we set off down this miserable path of cruelty, there appear to be good reasons. The cruelties are rarely (never?) portrayed as good of themselves. They are put forward as the means to a necessary and desirable end, or the just punishment or effective correction of error or betrayal. The new course is modern, is efficient, meets current needs and circumstances, will lead to a better place, produce in all a better result. Utopia beckons. How often have we heard this tale?

Of course, at the time a few wise counsellors will have expressed their conviction that the actions are wrong; and many will do so long after, when misery has run its course. What does such condemnation mean? This is a fundamental question.

A moral code

Is there such a thing as "wrong"? Is there an objective code of morality we should comply with? Can we properly describe some actions as innately "wrong", having a distinctive quality described as evil, or wicked ? Or is this mere emotion? Are we really saying, vigorously, that the action is inappropriate, did not result in the expected or beneficial result; or even that we find it deeply unattractive or repellent ourselves?

The distinction has ramifications. If we consider any action as innately "wrong", what is that judgement derived from? Where does an objective standard of right and wrong come from? If not, if terms like "wrong" are merely emotional responses, conveying disapproval or dislike, what general basis should we adopt for difficult decisions?

As a starting point, two observations. First, it is noticeable how keen we are to justify actions and policies by claiming they are "right" (and indeed, little less keen to condemn those we dislike as "wrong"). It seems that we mean (or at least feel) something more, and more powerful, than that they are correct or incorrect. We are not simply saying that the policy advocated is the cheapest, quickest, will work most efficiently. We seem to be claiming some moral justification for it. Is this mere intellectual laziness, merely inept use of English? No doubt those failings are often present, but there does seem to be something more.

The code - second nature?

There seems to be very deeply rooted in us a need to claim a consistency of our actions with a moral law. There also seems to be something deep within us which is far more affronted by what we regard as "wrong" than by what merely disadvantages us (unpleasant though that may be).

Consider how you would feel if turned down for a job because another candidate had a better academic record and experience; and alternatively that he was selected only because he was the CEO's nephew. The first case we would see as tough but fair; the second, as unjust, unfair, "wrong", and we would feel far more aggrieved.

Throughout history there is a consistency in view - across very different societies - as to what constitutes good, moral conduct. Unselfishness, loyalty, self-sacrifice, generosity, courage, help for your neighbours, honesty - all these appear again and again. These are not seen as good qualities because, in particular circumstances, they achieve some desirable end; they are seen as objectively good. They are not virtues by reference to something else, not virtues because (and only when and to the extent that) they assist efficiency, benefit the state, promote the organisation or even the family (or your own advancement). They stand alone.

This is not an antique emotion; we still feel it. We still recognise and strongly approve the Bishop helping Jean Valjean (*Les Misérables*), taking him in and then, having suffered his theft, giving him more. Later, we recognise the reformed Valjean's courage, loyalty and self-sacrifice, performed in great risk and facing the likelihood that the course chosen by him will result in his own suffering.

We are moved; we assent; why? What is the basis for our recognition of this "code" of unselfishness, "fair play", decent behaviour? Do we indeed recognise, measure behaviour against, an objective moral code, a natural law?

The fundamental point is whether we understand our approval or condemnation of conduct as "right" or "wrong" as a (perhaps unstated) recognition that there is, indeed, a valid, objective, moral code - or not.

An objectively true code

An objective morality implies that this code, these qualities, are always correct. They do not depend on legal recognition, or belief, or circumstances. They are, in a sense, factual - akin to the rule that 2+2 = 4. It does not matter that I do not know that 2+2 =4, or that I think the sum is 5. It is objectively true, true independent of my (or any other) view or recognition.

Or do we have some other answer? Perhaps these feelings are so changeable as to be too uncertain to form any "code" or natural law; or do they represent instincts which have evolved with us; or mere personal preferences; or are they responses developed from the teaching we have received "at our mother's knee"? Or are they merely rational choices about the most sensible way to run a society or to ensure its survival?

The view you come to is important, because a recognition of objective morality - a "code" of natural law - points to God, and also points to the traditional virtues recognised by Christianity (and other faiths).

Mutability (or not)

Reflection on ourselves and research into history gives some powerful support to the view that objective morality does exist. Far from different individuals, eras and cultures setting up different codes, there is a striking consistency. Where there are some apparent differences, these are often explained by circumstances. And, of course, we can readily accept that a consistent code may nevertheless be subject to different levels of insight among different individuals and societies. There will also be different ideas on how to apply it in practice. We may share a will to help our neighbour, but differ as to how to go about it. The important thing is our joint recognition of the duty. That is so widespread that it is hard to write off a "code" of objective morality as too various among different people(s) to be a credible possibility. It would be hard to find a society advocating cowardice, dishonesty and cruelty as virtues.

Instinct

Is this common response, this common appreciation of the same range of qualities making up a "code", merely the response of innate instinct, perhaps instinct honed by some evolutionary process? Perhaps societies with a sufficient number of people reacting like this flourished, expanded, so the trait spread?

These "instinctive" answers do not, on investigation, convince. Most of us will find that our instincts do not, in fact, reflect these qualities - they are directly opposed to them. The "code" is, broadly, about "unselfish" qualities. Yet I find that by instinct I usually wish to do selfish things. I have to overrule my instincts, take a deliberate (often reluctant) step in order to act in accordance with what I know is the "code". Instinctively, I wish to do things the "unselfish" code rejects, and to avoid what it commands. I do not think I am unusual in this.

An evolutionary explanation also looks weak. Those claiming we are improving often point to social and moral changes over the last 50 or 100 or 200 years - a tiny amount of time in evolutionary terms. Then again, who is to say we are improving? I read recently of Neanderthal remains from the Stone Age being discovered. They showed the marks of cannibalism. Some small group had attacked, killed and eaten another in time of famine. We recoil, and feel superior. Yet what was happening in Auschwitz seventy years ago? And that occurred without the excuse of threatened starvation for those ordering the killings. A moment's thought shows many other examples. Over time, things change - some for the better, some worse. Yet overall we do not seem to have good instincts, or be developing better ones.

Further, of course, we can hardly criticise people like the Nazis if they are, indeed, merely following their instincts. We may have to contend with them, but we cannot criticise them on moral grounds, any more than we would a man-eating tiger.

Personal preference

Is it all really a matter of taste? I like meat, you like fish; I like red, you like blue; no one is "right". We merely state personal preferences, and (where we feel strongly) seek to give our own tastes gravitas by inventing a concept of objective morality. There is no such thing; merely how you (or I) wish to behave.

There are two responses. The first is suggested by Mike Tyson's comment: "Everybody has a plan, 'til they get punched in the mouth". Only a clever and comfortable philosopher could think that, as he is punched to the ground and has his wallet stolen, his reaction will (or should) be "I do not approve of assault and robbery, but that is only my personal preference". So most of us certainly feel very strongly that the "code" is not a preference, but an objective reality.

The second is that while the code may (often will) overlap with our feelings, we regard it as something more. We consider the code applies, even if the law says otherwise; and even as regards individuals and governments electing to act counter to it: the Nazis (or Stalinists, or Pol Pot's regime, or many, many others).

So the "emotion" explanation does not fully cover our response. Indeed, even those inclined to the personal response view of morality often also incline to some areas of objective morality. They may regard, for example, tolerance as an objective good, to be properly demanded of all, including those who do not personally prefer to be tolerant.

Teaching

Have we imbibed these lessons at home, at school, at work, through social pressure? Again, one's personal experience leads to doubt. I recall learning the common law rule on title transfer and its exceptions at university ("Nemo dat quod non habet", No one gives what he does not have). But I do not feel about that as I feel about objective morality. Further, I have views on objective morality on matters never discussed at home, rarely or never at school, and developed (so far as I can recall) from innate conviction.

Reason

Could the code represent a rational decision, could we believe in these principles because experience has shown that they assist society to run smoothly? More problems here: the appreciation of this moral code certainly does not feel like a rational, reasoned matter. It is much more a gut feeling, an innate conviction. Indeed, reason is often on the other side, concocting justifications, exceptions, excuses, to allow us to ignore what we innately "know" we should do (or not do).

Secondly, while society as a whole may indeed benefit from honest dealing, or unselfishness, or other examples of the moral code, I may well perceive personal benefit in acting otherwise. If this is simply a matter of rationality, why should I not so act? Who can criticise me, on moral grounds, if these "feelings" are purely a collective judgement about effective practical operations - and I opt out for my own advantage?

Survival

Suppose we say that all the ingredients of the moral code are changeable, but within an overall purpose: the preservation of human society. Past examples of good conduct within the code may, or may not, remain valid in the future: it all depends on what is needed to preserve human society at that moment.

Again, this brings problems. Why should preserving human society be an objective principle? It certainly does not feel to be the basis for my reactions to the moral code. I feel I should be honest, because that is "right" - not because it will help society last another 20 (or more) generations. I fear I have little interest in distant posterity - certainly not the strong feelings I have for the moral code.

Yet the difficulty is that we feel this moral code strongly. That is a truth of history, and a reality today. Why else do we respond powerfully to the moral choices in *Les Misérables?* I believe we respond in this way because the action brings forward, in vivid ways, deep conflicts and convictions within us. Like Valjean, we are tempted to let the law take its course against the wretched vagrant arrested in his place, can think of rational justifications - and know we should not. Doing the right thing is often clear, rarely easy.

The source and purpose of the moral code

So what is the source of this moral code, this appreciation of objective good we feel so strongly? It is a reality; it influences our conduct; it is objective, not personally created; following, or denying it, influences our character - so it can be seen as having a purpose (to develop certain types of characteristics in us - to mould our soul).

The Christian answer (and the answer of other faiths) is that the moral code is implanted in us by God. Its nature reflects God's own nature, as a spirit of intelligence and power. The type of conduct reflected in the code is the type of conduct God's intelligence favours. The implanting in us reflects his power and purpose - to create humans sharing his character - persons in his image.

The concept of an objective moral code has a powerful link with the form of consciousness after death. So many visions and reports of "near death experiences" include some form of "audit", some complete review of everything in one's life, and its consequences. Indeed, our own experiences of the elderly and the experience of those who work with the dying, seem to share a similar pattern. A characteristic of an easier passing is acceptance, an abandonment of selfishness, a finding of love.

This is not the same as giving up our unique identity; but it does mean some "refining". We need to be filled with love, of God and neighbour. We need to let go of what we want; what we have; our priority of self-will; our preference for ourselves; our bitter determination to satisfy ourselves, our regret for what we have been denied. We need to trust God. In other words, we need to align ourselves with the very virtues, and give up the very vices, that the Christian Church (and other faiths) have long taught.

5.6 An aid in uncertainty: the asymmetric choice

Let us weigh the gain and the loss in wagering that God is. Let us estimate these two chances. If you gain, you gain all; if you lose, you lose nothing. Wager, then, without hesitation, that he is.

Blaise Pascal (1623-1662)

It is, of course, fair to note this: if you are sure there is no "life after death", you can ignore the issue of heaven and hell.

Given the potential consequences, you have to be sure. You must hold your opinion without doubt, and under conviction that you cannot be mistaken.

The reason is the asymmetric consequences of lives lived out according to the two beliefs.

If there is no life after death, you will never know you were right. There will be no consequences, after death, of your belief; no joy, and no pain.

But if there is life after death, the consequences of belief (or refusal to believe), and conduct in life, may be immense. Are you absolutely sure that there is no life after death, absolutely sure that you could not be mistaken, and absolutely sure that you have done all the research you can on the matter? If you cannot answer with an unqualified "yes", your house is built on sand. It would be madness not to investigate the matter further.

If you choose not to prepare for life after death, you will run great risks if it exists. If you prepare, and it does not exist, there are few consequences. The imbalance is such - and the consequences potentially so dramatic, in terms of joy or pain - that you need to be very sure before you say that you do not believe and act upon that conviction.

That imbalance is at the heart of Pascal's Wager. At the very least you need to research and reflect. You may come to entire conviction that there is no afterlife. If, however, you fall short of a complete conviction held without doubt, uncertainty, acknowledgement of an alternative possibility, then your route is clear. The inevitable choice of reason is to prepare for the afterlife.

5.7 Summary: what consciousness after death means

Then he said, "Jesus, remember me when you come into your kingdom." He answered him, "In truth I tell you, today you will be with me in paradise".

(*Lk* 23: 42-43)

Go forth, Christian soul, from this world in the name of God the almighty Father, who created you, in the name of Jesus Christ, the Son of the living God, who suffered for you, in the name of the Holy Spirit, who was poured out upon you. Go forth, faithful Christian! May you live in peace this day. May you be with God in Zion…

Prayer of Commendation for the Dying

The analysis of consciousness after death leads us to the following position. There are credible grounds to believe:

- That in some form the "imprint" of our character continues after our bodily death, and experiences some form of consciousness.

- That the experiences of that consciousness differ between different souls.

- That the difference is determined by choices made in life.

- That joy after death flows from an unselfish character, one of love and trust, formed in life; that misery flows from a character dominated by self love and self will.

- That the identification of conduct as "selfish" or "unselfish" flows from objective moral values.

- That the source of objective moral values is God.

- That, in coming to a view, we should sensibly and properly bear in mind the asymmetric nature of the consequences of a life lived in accord with belief, and one lived on the basis of unbelief, explained in Pascal's Wager.

- That acceptance of the fact - or even the likelihood or possibility - of consciousness after death and the other points noted in this paragraph brings us close indeed to beliefs long established and explained over the centuries by the Christian faith - in God, heaven, hell, sin, virtue and salvation.

6. Christian Fundamentals:
a Structural Summary

For at the judgement seat of Christ we are all to be seen for what we are, so that each of us may receive what he has deserved in the body, matched to whatever he has done, good or bad.

(2 Co 5:10)

6.1 Introduction

How poor a clod of earth is a manor! How poor an inch, a shire! How poor a span, a kingdom! And how poor a place, the whole world! And yet how prodigally we sell Paradise, Heaven, souls, consciences, immortality, eternity, for a few grains of this dust!

John Donne: *from a Sermon preached to the King's Majesty at Whitehall, 24th February, 1625*: quoted in *No Man Is An Island:* Rivers Scott

This chapter analyses some of the consequences of any form or degree of belief in a consciousness after death. Even something far short of belief - a "might be true" or "could not rule it out" - has consequences.

One is the importance of investigating further. Another is the interesting coincidence of certain ideas, fundamental themes shared by those who believe (or see as possible) consciousness after death, and an informed Christian - such as the effect of sin and virtue on the soul. This sharing prompts a consideration of certain Christian doctrines, explained over centuries by theologians and writers. A sophisticated understanding has been developed of key issues relating to our experience after death, of heaven and hell, and how we reach our destination. This learning is worth review and reflection.

Cultural hurdles

We need to be aware of some cultural hurdles in this review of shared ideas.

First, we are over-familiar with some of the language, can readily take short cuts and miss the fundamentals of some of the meanings.

Second, we can readily confuse the mundane daily activities of the Church - the fêtes and fundraisings, the socials, the visits, even the public statements on current issues - with a dramatic, powerful, unseen world of spiritual reality. It is that spiritual reality we will encounter on our bodily death. Our preparedness will depend on our life on earth. That is why sin and virtue, choice and thought, word and deed, are so important.

Thinking about the impact of sin is not some smirking reference to how you ramped your expenses or might make hay with that striking blonde from Accounts at, or after, the office party. It is a terrifying analysis of how frail man can succeed in severing himself eternally even from the unending love of an almighty God. It really is not a laughing matter.

6.2 Heaven: untrammelled good

He then said, "Please show me your glory". Yahweh said," I shall make all my goodness pass before you, and before you I shall pronounce the name Yahweh…But my face," he said, "you cannot see, for no human being can see me and survive".

(Ex 33:18-21)

Your eyes are too pure to rest on evil.

(Hab 1:13)

…the king of kings and lord of lords,
Who alone is immortal, whose home is in inaccessible light,
Whom no human being has seen or is able to see:
To him be honour and everlasting power.

(1 Tm 6:16)

Seek peace with all people, and the holiness without which no one can see the Lord.

(Heb 12:14)

God is all good, all wise, omnipotent. In some manner difficult to describe, he has created and is present in (though not limited by) heaven. All in heaven have some direct relationship with, some vision of, God.

While the lesser than God can happily dwell in heaven, the inconsistent cannot. The reason is that God's "all goodness" and omnipotence cannot co-exist alongside "ungoodness". Any such meeting would limit the filling of heaven with "all goodness" through omnipotence, which is a logical impossibility.

By the presence of God, heaven is all good. Nothing less than good can survive in heaven. Anyone who wishes to come to heaven must be willing to give up all elements of "ungoodness". No creature which sought to retain any "ungoodness" could survive God's presence in heaven (or would wish to seek to do so). That principle, of a willingness to give up our "ungoodness", is fundamental to understanding how we can come to heaven - and, terribly, how we could elect never to do so.

6.3 Our unfitness for heaven

Good master, what must I do to inherit eternal life ? Jesus said to him, "Why do you call me good ? No one is good but God alone. You know the commandments: You shall not kill; you shall not commit adultery; you shall not steal; you shall not give false witness; you shall not defraud; honour your father and mother.

(*Mk* 10:17-20)

You have heard how it was said, You shall not commit adultery. But I say this to you, if a man looks at a woman lustfully, he has already committed adultery with her in his heart. If your right eye should be your downfall, tear it out and throw it away; for it will do you less harm to lose one part of yourself than to have your whole body thrown into hell.

(Mt 5:27-30)

Do you sometimes sit or kneel alone in an empty church, and gaze on a large crucifix or cross near the altar? Are you appalled, struck by the immeasurable gulf between you and God?

Suppose it's all true: that God exists, Jesus is God, the events recorded in the New Testament did, indeed, occur. Just suppose for a moment. Reflect on this completely good, wise, courageous and honest man, Jesus. A man who healed the sick, who showed mercy, who gave good advice, who tried to help.

And look at what men did to him - tortured him to death, because of their arrogance, folly, worldly position, fear of change, fear of the unplanned and unknown, preference for established forms and order over truth and love.

Who are we closer to, by nature and inclination, by the evidence of our past conduct? To Jesus - or to the Pharisees, the Sadducees, the Temple officials and the mob?

Are we minded to dissent from that categorisation? To assert that we are not that bad, not violent, not prone to complicity in the death of the innocent?

Consider. Did you enjoy your last holiday? What car do you drive? Do you take pleasure in your house and interest in its decoration and furnishings? Do you have plans for future expenditure? Do you enjoy the status and authority of your job?

Yet we all well know that there are many people in the world desperately poor, living lives made miserable by want, some starving. We know well there are charities operating to relieve this suffering, and we know how to make donations to them. Yet we choose not to, or not to do so until we have satisfied ourselves to a level unimaginable and unattainable for those poor, starving neighbours.

We have a lot to learn from the Biblical widow and her mite. We give only from our surplus, and pay out much for inconsequential pleasures long before we are prepared to recognise that surplus.

A few moments of thought, a little self-knowledge, brings a grim awakening. We love our will. We are selfish. We are proud. We do unkind things because we choose to do them. We refrain from charity by choice. We put ourselves first. We flatter for advantage, disdain for pleasure. We lack courage and charity, by nature and choice. As we stand now, on our own, without help, we are unfitted for heaven.

6.4 The need and fact of a saviour

So then, no human being can be found upright at the tribunal of God by keeping the Law; all that the Law does is to tell us what is sinful.

(*Rm* 3:20)

Just as by one man's disobedience many were made sinners, so by one man's obedience are many to be made upright. When Law came on the scene, it was to multiply the offences. But however much sin increased, grace was always greater; so that as sin's reign brought death, so grace was to rule through saving justice that leads to eternal life through Jesus Christ our Lord.

(Rm 5:19-21)

Without more, our case would be hopeless. Even if there is consciousness after death, even if heaven exists, we could never arrive in such a destination on our own. Even the best of us is inclined to (and will) sin. That history and character is part of us. But no evil can exist in the presence of God in heaven. So none of us could ever enter heaven.

We depend entirely on some external help to resolve the impasse - a saviour. That saviour is Jesus. It is his life and death that reconciles us with God, makes it possible for us to enter heaven. We know this from His own words; from the words of His apostles; from the teaching of the Christian Church over the centuries (in all its denominations), and from the writings and lives of mystics and religious.

6.5 The effect of the Resurrection

In all truth I tell you, whoever keeps my word will never see death.

(Jn 8:51)

The sheep that belong to me listen to my voice; I know them and they follow me, I give them eternal life; they will never be lost.

(Jn 10:27-28)

There is much evidence for the resurrection: the empty tomb; the meetings of Jesus sometimes with one or few, sometimes with many; the words of Jesus and his actions (eating, walking, speaking); the dramatic impact upon a disheartened group of eleven disciples, who go on to lives of witness and sacrifice (all, or all but one, are martyred).

The resurrection nevertheless remains a mystery. The effect of the resurrection for us is described by metaphor, by analogy with human society. Familiar phrases speak of ransom; of paying our debts; of bearing our punishment; of taking on our sins. These descriptions will help some come to terms with the concept. The author himself finds them of limited assistance, preferring to accept the simple fact of Jesus's resurrection and our salvation. Many of us are content to drive our cars without understanding the mechanics of the engine.

The fundamentals remain. It is the resurrection which is key to the Christian faith. It is the resurrection which confirms all Jesus's works and teachings. It confirms his divinity and confirms the promises he made of our salvation.

6.6 Two cautions: we sin and sin matters

No, the arm of Yahweh is not too short to save, nor his ear too dull to hear. But your guilty deeds have made a gulf between you and your God.

(Is 59:2)

If we say, "We have no sin", we are deceiving ourselves and truth has no place in us.

(1 Jn 1:8)

For the wage paid by sin is death; the gift freely given by God is eternal life in Christ Jesus our Lord.

(Rm 6:23)

Jesus has saved us; so can we go on sinning with impunity? If he has taken on our sins, perhaps it does not matter how many we have - all are discharged, paid for, however serious and numerous. Perhaps they have no effect at all?

The response, of course, is that our sins matter very much. Jesus has made it possible for us to enter heaven despite our fallen nature - the nature that results, however hard we try, in our sinning.

But the possibility of entry into heaven is not the fact of entry into heaven. We still have our part to play. We still have to choose heaven. The problem with sin is that it will make that choice difficult.

The choice and the act

Can a tortoise fly? Imagine a highly intelligent tortoise attempting the task. Unfortunately, no amount of effort or training will permit take off. Then, suddenly, a private jet lands on the runway beside the tortoise. A gently sloping ramp is lowered. All the tortoise has to do is walk up it - something readily within his capabilities. Everything difficult has been done, and freely, for him. But the choice, and act, still have to be made and carried out. The tortoise can always refuse, and his refusal will be respected.

The choice for us is a simple one: to come to God, and heaven, or not.

The legacy of sin

Sin is relevant to our choice in two ways. First (and most important) our sins in life will shape our soul, and it is our soul that makes the choice. Second, the barriers to God in our soul, created by sin, will have to be cast away before we can enjoy heaven.

It is not each of our sins in itself which most matters, but its effect on us. Not so much the lie we tell, or the fact that we have told a lie. It is the fact that slowly and steadily we become a liar. A part of our character acquires a new element: that of being a liar. And it loses something else: an element of honesty and trustworthiness. Those changes become engrafted in us, become part of our soul.

That effect of sin makes us more likely to refuse to come to God, and heaven. It is tellingly described in the Bible, as a hardening of heart, making us stiff-necked, making us unwilling to bend the knee even to God. Sin inclines us to preserve our priority of self, even in the face of God, even at the cost of heaven.

The second effect of sin is less serious, but still significant. Even if we can still choose God, our sin has left a mark in our soul, a barrier, something inconsistent with heaven. That mark - that part of selfishness in our soul - needs to be pared away, with our full consent, before we can rest in heaven. That is the process of purgatory.

That paring away will not be an elegant matter, not a case of allowing, as it were, a silk handkerchief to flutter gently to the ground. It will be a hard and brutal case of cutting out or burning away that very part of us which is unfitted for heaven. It can only be done with our consent. We have to understand what is, what we are, what we must give up - and choose. The process of purging will not be easy.

6.7 Hell: the inevitable corollary of freedom

We cannot be united with God unless we freely choose to love him. But we cannot love God if we sin gravely against him, against our neighbour or against ourselves…To die in mortal sin without repenting and accepting God's merciful love means remaining separated from him for ever by our own free choice. This state of definitive self exclusion from communion with God and the blessed is called "Hell".

Catechism of the Catholic Church, Para 1033

If we refuse to come to God, in heaven, something must happen to us. That something is to retain our consciousness outside heaven. We have chosen selfishness, the priority of our will, so we will live with it. We will do so knowing what we might have had - the eternal joy of heaven.

The sufferings in hell have clear (albeit much lesser) analogies in this life. We only have to reflect for a moment on our own life, and on missed chances to do good, wrong choices, opportunities wasted, mistakes made, advantage taken of weakness.

Those thoughts can be bitter indeed, even with our limited memories, restricted understanding of the injuries we have done, and our general indulgence to ourselves. Think of the pain of knowing, and understanding in every detail, how we so misshaped our soul in life. Think of the pain of realisation that our free choices shaped a soul that chose against God and the bliss of heaven at the moment of death. Think of the pain of enduring that reflection, in full detail, forever. No change, no respite, no alternative. Agony indeed.

7. Looking Ahead:
the Nature of Heaven and Hell

Of this each man and woman who desires to live contemplatively needs to have knowledge of the littleness of creatures and to like as nought all things that are made, for to love and have God who is unmade. For this is the cause why we be not all in ease of heart and soul, for we who are occupied wilfully in earthly business and evermore seek worldly weal are not heirs of his in heart and in soul for to live and to seek here rest, in these things that are so little wherein is no rest, and know not our God who is all mighty, all wise, all good. For he is the very rest. God will be known and he likes us to rest in him, for all that is beneath him does not suffice us. And this is the cause why no soul is rested, until it is noughted of all things that are made.

Revelations of Divine Love [Chapter 5]:
Julian of Norwich (c. 1342-1416)

7.1 Introduction: a prompt to action

[Wisdom] is a breath of the power of God, pure emanation of the glory of the Almighty; so nothing impure can find its way into her. For she is a reflection of the eternal light, untarnished mirror of God's active power, and image of his goodness. Although she is alone, she can do everything.

(*Ws* 7:25-27)

We spend time with holiday brochures, house particulars, catalogues, when considering a purchase. We reflect. Our imagination engages with the prospect, and prompts and reinforces our will.

So it should be with heaven - and hell. As we are more informed, see and understand those destinations more clearly, so our resolve is strengthened.

Hence the value of considering the picture presented by the Bible, Church teaching and revelation. Reflection and understanding prompt us to act, remind us of consequences.

7.2 Pictures, images, culture

But Stephen, filled with the Holy Spirit, gazed into Heaven and saw the glory of God, and Jesus standing at God's right hand. "Look! I can see heaven thrown open," he said, "and the Son of Man standing at the right hand of God."

(*Ac* 7:55-57)

Mostly, we think in words. We can, of course, think in other ways - figures, diagrams, pictures. But mostly, it is words. They work well. They are especially useful for grouping, comparing and for swift categorization. But they have their dangers. The slippery politician, the clever salesman, know well how to obscure the truth, arouse emotion, blur valid distinctions, present unsustained conclusions. And the rest of us, less agile in the skill but no more worthy, follow their example.

Even when we do our best, we make mistakes. Our logic is faulty - it stops short, or has gaps. Our imagination is too limited. We are too much influenced by the culture of our day, our personal experiences (especially recent ones). Above all, we seek to explain matters by analogy, by linking the matter in issue with familiar but different experiences which nevertheless appear to have some similarities.

We are also prone to taint thought with emotion, judgement with personal preference.

We are readily inclined to describe God in a way to suit us, not God. We emphasise the sins we dislike, destine for elaborate torture in a hell we design the people we despise or fear, those who hold views we hate. All too readily, our sinfulness and selfishness start to colour our picture of God.

We need to be aware of the tendency, of each one of us, to let inclination press upon judgement.

We also need to bear in mind a countervailing danger. The (legitimate) criticism of our inaccuracy is not an argument against the reality we were seeking to describe. It is a truthful, painful acknowledgment of the nature of mankind, and a recognition of our own weakness. It should prompt us to humility. But the fact that we describe God or heaven ineptly does not mean each is less than real.

We need to be conscious of this unfortunate inclination to err both in making our own pictures, and in studying the works of earlier generations. We all use language, pictures, metaphor linked to our prevailing culture, and tending to be misshaped by the errors of that culture, and of our character. Earlier metaphors sometimes carry little impact for a later, very different, culture. They may even be misleading, absurd or off-putting. The Biblical widow prays to come before a just judge, a powerful image in an era of corrupt officialdom and overwhelming individual power. But a reader in Britain today takes the justice of a judge largely for granted. They hope instead not to come before a judge at all, or for a merciful judge.

Hellfire: a metaphor?

Even the flames of hell - a terrible warning indeed - can now appear absurd or grotesque. But we have not stood by St Mary's Gate, close to Gloucester Cathedral, on the cold and windy morning of 9th February 1555. We have not seen Bishop John Hooper die in agony at the stake, the fire lit three times, the burning taking 45 minutes. Nor have we been in Gloucester again, this time on 11th August 1586, to see the end of the Catholic martyr the Blessed John Sandys, cut down from hanging while fully conscious, his stomach cut open with a rusty and ragged knife, his entrails drawn out while he still lived and prayed for his persecutors.

We have not felt the heat, smelt the burning flesh and the fresh blood, heard the cries. We have not turned away, perhaps feeling less satisfied than we hoped, more reluctantly impressed than we dare admit.

Another world, different images.

So the first step in a clear understanding of heaven and hell is to appreciate the distinction between image and reality. An image made by a particular human mind in a particular human society, may (or may not) be helpful to illuminate a truth when new minted, or later. If unhelpful, it can be laid aside. That laying aside of image in no way affects the underlying reality it seeks to describe.

7.3 Three Heavens: Heaven on Earth, the Present Heaven, Heaven after the Final Judgement

Finally, brothers, let your minds be filled with everything that is true, everything that is honourable, everything that is upright and pure, everything that we love and admire - with whatever is good and praiseworthy. Keep doing everything you learnt from me and were told by me and have heard or seen me doing. Then the God of peace will be with you.

(*Ph* 4:8-9)

We use "heaven" (or phrases like "the kingdom of heaven", or "the kingdom of God") for three different, though related, cases.

The FIRST meaning is that we can, in some ways, become aware of, even part of, God's kingdom while still living our life on earth.

The SECOND meaning is the familiar one, of being with God in heaven after our death.

The THIRD meaning is being with God in the new heaven and the new earth, after the Final Judgement. Clearly, there are important similarities - in experiencing deep peace, love, understanding and the presence of God. But they are not the same, and the distinctions need to be borne in mind.

7.4 Heaven on earth

We have to work very hard indeed to get contemplative sweetness, but when we do get it the joy is unbelievable. Of course it is not something that we can win by our own merit, but God's gift, and never yet, from the beginning of the world to this very day, has anyone ever been ravished in the contemplation of Everlasting Love without completely giving up the vanities of this world.

Contemplation: Richard Rolle (1300-1349): quoted in *The Way of the English Mystics:* Gordon L. Miller

So let us pause here, my sisters, and beg the Lord that, since to some extent it is possible for us to enjoy heaven on earth, he will grant us his help so that it will not be our fault if we miss anything...

Interior Castle: The Fifth Mansion:
St Teresa of Avila (1515-1582)

Then in the spring of 1925, if I remember correctly, when I was taking a walk in the garden by myself, I felt that the universe suddenly quaked, and that a golden spirit sprang up from the ground, veiled my body, and changed my body into a golden one. At the same time my mind and body became light. I was able to understand the whispering of the birds, and was clearly aware of the mind of God, the creator of the universe. At that moment I was enlightened: the source of budo is God's love the spirit of loving protection for all beings. Endless tears of joy streamed down my cheeks.

Morihei Ueshiba (1883-1969), founder of the martial
art Aikido: quoted in *Aikido* by Kisshomaru Ueshiba

God created everything that is, and holds it in existence.

There is no satisfactory earthly parallel for this role. Nevertheless, as it is useful to describe it in a succinct and familiar way, traditionally terms like "King" , "Ruler", "Owner" have been adopted. They have merits of speed and convenience, but fall far short of reality.

The concept of a kingdom prompts the analogy of mankind as subjects, more or less loyal, diligent, rebellious, ignorant. We are all subjects, whether we acknowledge it or not. Those who appreciate and consent to follow the kingdom structure, the will of the king and his purpose, understand more. They find their mind in tune with fundamental realities. Their daily experience in the world is consistent with their philosophy, their understanding of fundamental realities. That all brings content.

There is more. We can find some degree of joy in this world - through its natural beauty, through proper employment of our skill, through charity, through prayer and meditation on God, through the Eucharist. In general, even in this fallen world, contemplation of God and his works brings peace, joy and power. Paul refers to this in his letter to the Corinthians (*1 Co* 3:21-23).

The experiences of mystics, religious, people we might regard as exceptionally good or saints, testifies to this. History (and, for many of us, our own experience) shows that there is available, though limited and episodic, even during our life on earth:

- An encompassing sense of peace;
- A sense of the world as part of an ordered creation, made and sustained with love and purpose;
- Power to effect change through prayer - to work miracles;
- Power of prophecy and interpretation;

- Joy prompted by the beauty and value of the natural creation;
- Awe of the power and love of God;
- Understanding of the value and individuality of every human, and their potential on earth and eternally.

In this life, these joys and powers, this peace, are inevitably limited in extent and degree. We still wrestle - and by no means always successfully - with a sinful nature and the snares of Satan. But we see enough to give a real hope and awareness of the future.

7.5 The present heaven

...it is as Scripture says: What no eye has seen and no ear has heard, what the mind of man cannot visualize, all that God has prepared for those who love him, to us, though, God has given revelation through the Spirit, for the Spirit explores the depths of everything, even the depths of God.

(1 Co 2: 9)

How great will your glory and happiness be, to be allowed to see God, be honoured with sharing the joy of salvation and eternal light with Christ your Lord and God...to delight in the joy of immortality in the kingdom of heaven - with the righteous and God's friends.

St Cyprian (c. 200-258)

My idea of heaven is driving in a post chaise with a pretty woman, eating pate de foie gras to the sound of trumpets.

Rev. Sydney Smith (1771-1845)

When I get to heaven I mean to spend a considerable portion of my first million years in painting, and so get to the bottom of the subject. But then I shall require a still gayer palette than I get here below. I expect orange and vermillion will be the darkest, dullest colours upon it, and beyond them there will be a whole range of wonderful new colours which will delight the celestial eye.

Painting as a Pastime: Winston S. Churchill
(1874-1965)

Upon our death, we receive our "particular judgement". We pass to our irrevocable destination, heaven or hell. So far, all who have died and gone to heaven have arrived at the present heaven: the heaven that exists in our terms "now".

While some theologians have speculated on a period of "sleep" between death and Final Judgement, the words of Jesus and the teaching of the Church are otherwise. These indicate a present heaven in which we have a form of consciousness and experience joy.

Heaven is not in the sky. We will not find it by sending space craft ever further into the universe. It is a different thing, a different dimension. Our concepts of time, gravity, light, space may have parallels there, but there is no reason to suppose that exactly comparable features exist in heaven. Interestingly, modern physics, approaching as it were from a different direction, also speculates on the existence of other dimensions beyond those we experience in this world.

We have been told some things about this present heaven. We can deduce others. Mystics and visionaries have spoken about it. But we need to bear in mind the words of the Bible, its caution and its encouragement. Heaven is not simply a fairer, sleeker, smarter version of earth. It is something better - and different.

We are, however, able to discern enough for our profound encouragement.

Characteristics of heaven

GOD: The first, and most important, feature is that we will have a direct sight of God and a direct relationship with God. We will feel and know God's complete, unlimited, unchanging, love for us (*Jo* 19: 25-26; *1 Co* 11-12). All the other joy and fulfilment of heaven flows from this.

PEACE: We will have no fear, no anxiety, no uncertainty. We will know that we are free, forever, from bad news, cruelty, illness, disappointment. We will know continually God's unending and complete love for our distinct soul, and know that such love will never change.

SELF-WORTH: Each one of us will fully understand, fully take to heart that God created us deliberately and distinctly. We are honoured by being individually chosen for a unique and valuable purpose. We will see that our soul, individual and different from all others, was made because it alone could have a specific relationship with God. That relationship is unique. Each of us will understand that no one else can have our relationship with God. Each of us was created to fulfil that purpose. If any of us fails, no one else can perform their specific function.

GRATITUDE: We will see fully how God created us, guided, helped and saved us. We will see how our Guardian Angel and our friends, family, others, all helped us form our souls to the point at which they stood at death, and so helped us come to heaven.

FORGIVENESS: We will experience - and fully understand and feel - the wonderful reality of forgiveness. We will be able to forgive all who injured us; and we will know that we ourselves are forgiven for all our selfishness, follies, sin, mistakes. Every thought, word or deed of ours which departed from the true path we should have followed, is forgiven. We need no more feel ashamed. It is washed away. We may even see all our sins as mere nothingness, causing pain indeed, but causing us to know ourselves and to be purged (Julian of Norwich, *The Thirteenth Revelation*).

JOY: We will be filled with an unending joy as we observe that, after all the trials of life, we have indeed come to the haven and relationship for which we were always created.

INTEREST: God is infinite. We have unending exploration before us, all filled with fascination, novelty and happiness. The exploration and its discoveries are all exactly suited to our own soul.

FULFILMENT: We will find that the fundamental longing we experienced in this world is fulfilled. Most of us, in life, will have sought to satisfy those deep feelings of need in material ways. We will have sought wealth or power, position, reputation, or the ownership of particular assets, or the pursuit of particular interests, or the stimulation of particular senses. Most of us will have found our ambitions unrealised. Those, an apparently fortunate few, who achieve their ambitions will find that, somehow, the fundamental need remains unfulfilled. The wrapping was better than the present. But in heaven we will receive the complete fulfilment of that inner, fundamental need.

How will we experience heaven?

It seems that we will have some form of appearance, which can in some way understand, prompted by impulses akin to sight, hearing, thought, emotion. However, since heaven is outside our universe, these forms of appreciation do not require the eyes, ears or brain that we have on earth. Nor do they require the same stimulus that we found for joy on earth.

It may be that there will be grass, trees, rivers, mountains; music and literature; mathematics, languages and architecture, but all far more impressive than on earth, and our appreciation far more direct. Perhaps Sydney Smith and Churchill had an inkling of it. But it may be quite different; in place of what we have seen on earth, something far more absorbing and satisfying for us.

We do not know.

But the effect (and our reaction and involvement) will be far more intense, far more real, sustained and unalloyed than with their counterparts on earth. We are not going to something lesser, something less fit for our enjoyment; we are arriving where we are designed to be. The experiences will exactly meet, in full, all our individual needs and desires. We will want for nothing, have no unfulfilled desire. We will be changed.

We have an inkling of this even in our life on earth. When I was a schoolboy, a high point of happiness was numberless games of football. We were so absorbed that, even after a formal match, we would continue with an informal "kick around" until driven in by darkness. But tastes change. Other prompts now give a sense of joy and fulfilment. The important point is the fact of the joy, not the nature of the prompt. If we experience that joy - and in intense degree and without interruption - we will not hunger for any of those old, outmoded forms which were apt as prompts to our earthly happiness.

7.6 Heaven after the Final Judgement

The day of the Lord will come like a thief, and then with a roar the sky will vanish, the elements will catch fire and melt away, the earth and all that it contains will be burned up...What we are waiting for, relying on his promises, is the new heavens and new earth, where uprightness will be at home.

(2 P 10:13)

My dear friends, we are already God's children, but what we shall be in the future has not yet been revealed. We are well aware that when he appears. We shall be like him, Because we shall see him as he really is.

(1 Jn 3:2)

Then I saw a new heaven and a new earth; the first heaven and the first earth had disappeared now, and there was no longer any sea. I saw the holy city, the new Jerusalem, coming down out of heaven from God, prepared as a bride for her husband. Then I heard a loud voice call from the throne, "Look, here God lives among human beings. He will make his home among them; they will be his people, and he will be their God, God - With - Them. He will wipe away all tears from their eyes; there will be no more death, and no more mourning or sadness or pain. The world of the past has gone.

(Rv 21:1)

At some point will come the Final Judgement. Upon that, we will receive our resurrected bodies, and live on the new earth. This will be heavenly, in the sense that God will be present there. It will include a great city, the new Jerusalem. It will be eternal.

The Final Judgement completes the history of our earth and universe, and mankind upon it. The consequences of all things, all acts, words and deeds, will be made clear. The plan of God for our salvation, and how it has unfolded and worked out, will be made plain.

Together with this making clear, there will be a making new. The visible universe will be transformed into a new heaven and a new earth.

We will continue to enjoy the presence of God, and have all the joy and fulfilment of the present heaven, described above.

We will also have something more: we will have resurrected bodies. By possessing these, we will have additional scope for joy. The new earth - and our resurrected bodies - will be perfected versions of our familiar earth and bodies, and God will be present in the new earth.

7.7 Hell

And if your eye should be your downfall, tear it out; it is better for you to enter into the kingdom of God with one eye, than to have two eyes and be thrown into hell where their worm will never die nor their fire be put out.

(*Mk* 9:47-48)

The fact is that I don't know how to give a sufficiently powerful description of that interior fire and that despair coming in addition to such extreme torments and pains. I didn't see who inflicted them on me, but, as it seemed to me, I felt myself burning and crumbling; and I repeat the worst was that interior fire and despair.

On Her Vision of Hell: St Teresa of Avila (1515-1582)

I do not know what I am not ready to endure to avoid hell, in spite of my fear of pain. I see clearly that all the sufferings of earth are nothing in comparison with the horror of no longer being able to love, for in that place all breathes hatred and thirst to damn other souls.

> Sr Josefa Menéndez (1890-1923); Quoted in
> *Inside Heaven and Hell* by Thomas W. Petrisko

Hell is a prospect to appal and revolt. Reading about it, thinking about it, writing about it, is a sickening experience. But it cannot be ignored. If true, people must be warned. If true, it adds a terrible urgency to our need to choose our path to heaven.

It seems that - long before Christianity - mankind received insights into the existence and horrors of hell. Those insights have continued up to the present day. The concept of a place of punishment for the wicked after death apparently forms part of the beliefs of ancient Egypt, Greece, the Celts, the Slavs, Hindus, Christians, Muslims and the Mayans - just some examples. For Christians, these early insights, this dawning realisation of truth, is seen as part of the work of the Holy Spirit.

Jesus speaks on a number of occasions of hell. The Church from its earliest days has taught its reality.

Some of us have a deep-seated understanding that hell exists; some think it a possibility; some are full of denial, sceptical of descriptions seemingly "medieval", of torments inconceivable to civilised people let alone to a loving God.

If you are unsure, or think it may exist, reflect on the consequences of that view. It is an acceptance that this hideous prospect may indeed be the reality. Be aware that any uncertainty of ours does not affect the quality of hell, if hell exists. Hell is not watered down by our uncertainty. It's like risk. A 10% risk of a 100% loss is a serious concern - the low likelihood does not ameliorate the savage extent of loss, should it occur. If hell exists at all, it does so in the whole terrible nature of which we are warned.

Separation

The fundamental pain of hell is separation from God. Each soul in hell will understand that, throughout their lives on earth, they shaped their own soul in such a form that it chose hell. They will understand that such a work of ruin was made by their own freely exercised decisions in life. They were always free to make different choices. They will comprehend that their true destiny was heaven, and a unique relationship with God; and only that would have given them peace and joy.

The inferno

Jesus refers to hell as a place of fire and destruction, with souls in hell wailing, gnashing their teeth and suffering agonizing thirst. Is this metaphor or a literal description? Is the unending anguish of separation from God so terrible that, to convey its meaning to those on earth, being burnt is the best description? Or are there flames indeed?

St Augustine stated that the flames were real, and the *Catechism of the Catholic Church* (para 1034-1035) refers to the punishments of hell, 'eternal fire'. Certainly countless visions of hell have reported darkness, flames, cries, loneliness, unending misery. There is no relief, no companionship, no trust, no hope. Only pain, despair, regret.

The three forms of hell

Hell, like heaven, can be understood in three forms: first, experienced in lives on earth; second, the hell that exists for those who die now; and third, the hell that exists after the Final Judgement.

So many biographies about (at least to human judgement) evil lives, show individuals who, notwithstanding wealth and power, experienced a foretaste of the pains of hell - bitterness, despair, hatred, fear, loneliness, lack of any joy, trust or love.

The hell awaiting those who die now is described in the Bible and by visionaries as a place of extraordinary pain.

The hell after the Final Judgement is described as a lake of burning sulphur and brimstone, where the souls in hell, and Satan and the fallen angels, will reside and suffer (*Rv* 20:9).

Do not be deluded by the absurd comments of ill-informed comedians or pub bores. Hell is no place of fun, no place of sin persisted in or roguish jollity. It is no place of companionship with the like-minded. If it exists, it is terrible. All steps are to be taken to avoid it.

8. How We Shape Our Soul: Sin, Faith, Works

And so I tell you, every human sin and blasphemy will be forgiven, but blasphemy against the Spirit will not be forgiven. And anyone who says a word against the Son of man will be forgiven; but no one who speaks against the Holy Spirit will be forgiven either in this world or the next.

(Mt 12:31-32)

8.1 Sin

Sin is an offence against reason, truth and right conscience; it is failure in genuine love for God and neighbour caused by a perverse attachment to certain goods.

Catechism of the Catholic Church: para 1849

The movement of repentance involves the determination to make God and his will the guiding principle of life and the struggle to renounce idolatries, the undue attachment to relative goods, such as pleasure, popularity and success, which interfere with the Godward journey.

C. Jones, G. Wainwright,
E. Yarnold, eds, *The Study of Spirituality*

There are many kinds and classifications of sin. A traditional categorisation is between mortal and venial sins. Mortal sins are those whose object is grave matter and which are committed with full knowledge and deliberate consent (John Paul II, *Reconciliatio et Paenitentia* 17. 12, quoted in the *Catechism of the Catholic Church*, para 1857). Venial sins are less serious, and less damaging to us, in lacking one or more of these three elements (grave matter, full knowledge, deliberate consent).

Mortal sin may in practice be hard for most of us to commit, but its consequences are terrible. If unrepented (and so unforgiven in life) its effect on us is such that we will not come to heaven. Venial sin weakens our charity, our progress in virtue. It will result in pain for us, but does not bar us from heaven.

Another insightful categorisation is of capital sins (the seven deadly sins). These are pride; avarice; envy; wrath; lust; gluttony; sloth. They are described as capital because of their tendency to engender other sins.

Selfishness and sin

The quality of any act (or thought or word) depends on its object, intention and circumstances. Each of the three must avoid sin, but the quality of the act depends on all three. The fundamental quality is determined by the object of the act; but circumstances and intention reduce or increase the intensity of that quality, for good or ill.

The heart of every sin is selfishness. Each individual sin is prompted by the desire to put ourselves first, to make our preference prevail, to satisfy our desire, our will, at the cost of others or without regard to the harm arising for others.

The consequences of sin

All sin shares a character with the temptation of Adam and Eve. It is a willing response to the suggestion that we can be like gods - we can have untrammelled power to do whatever we please, without reference to the interest of others.

Sin, like a stone thrown into a pond, causes ripples - has consequences.

We may well neither anticipate nor, in our lifetime, know the full consequences. One selfish act of ours may have innumerable effects, on a number of people, over many years. We should tremble at the possible unfolding of the misery we cause by our self-indulgence. And there is no guarantee - unlike the ripples from the flung stone - that the adverse consequences will decline in severity as they move away from us in time or operate indirectly in effect.

The first and primary effect of sin is, however, on the sinner. Every act, or thought, or word of ours contributes to shaping our soul. It does so in two ways. Directly, each such event adds a grain of material, as it were, possibly insignificant in itself, but real nevertheless.

A second effect of sin is that it conditions us, increasing our ability to act further along the same lines. Each sin makes the next sin easier, just as each act of unselfishness makes the next good work easier.

There is an obvious parallel with our experience of work or exercise. We become more skilled, fitter and stronger as we work and exercise; we decline mentally and physically as we do less and eat more.

Choice and repentance

Our opportunities to shape our soul do not depend on intelligence, or skill, or personality, or success, or background, or strength. Indeed, the foetus, the infant, the very young child, may well be likely - perhaps certain - to come to heaven. One can readily envisage that each would show a simple desire for God.

For the rest of us, our peril grows with our years. As our powers increase, the opportunity for selfishness grows. We can increasingly choose self over God, and (mis)shape our soul by those choices.

Of course, there is the lifeline of repentance. Our sin can be wholly remitted - removed as far as East is from West - if we repent. In our Catholic Church, that takes the form of Confession or Reconciliation. But it is only effective if genuine; and genuine repentance means a full turning away from the choice of sin. It is not a coin in a slot; it is a matter of heart and mind. The pictures from the Old Testament, of rending garments, of sackcloth and ashes, of tears and lamentation, indicate the depth of feeling characteristic of true repentance.

The choice of the soul

The state of our soul is important - indeed, fundamental - because it is our soul which makes the decision, immediately on death, to come to God (and heaven) - or not.

If, through our life, we have gradually (and with whatever movements within the general trend, forward and back, in repentance and sin) shaped a soul which cannot accept God and heaven as they are, we will not get there. And we cannot change the shape of our soul after death. What it is then, it is. We cannot take revision notes into the examination hall. As we come to the doors, what we are is all we have from which to make our answer.

8.2 Faith

I believe in one God,
The Father almighty,
Maker of heaven and earth,
Of all things visible and invisible.

The Nicene Creed

Believing is an act of the intellect assenting to the divine truth by command of the will moved by God through grace.

St Thomas Aquinas (1225-1274) quoted in the
Catechism of the Catholic Church, para 155

The Nicene Creed stems from the first two ecumenical councils of the Christian Church, held in 325 and 381 AD. It remains a commonly held basis of belief for all main Christian denominations to this day.

Faith is the personal loyalty or commitment of an individual to God, and to the truths revealed by God.

Faith is based on a gift of God, enabling us to open our heart and mind to this conviction; and in our will, in choosing to trust the truths of and concerning God.

Faith leads to salvation. This must be, since the change of heart associated with a genuine faith is a guarantee of love of God and neighbour, and a rejection of the priority of self:

> Anyone who believes in the Son has eternal life,
> But anyone who refuses to believe in the Son will
> never see life: God's retribution hangs over him.
>
> *(Jn 3:36)*

Genuine faith is, however, more than belief alone.

> You believe in the one God - that is creditable enough, but even the demons have the same belief, and they tremble with fear. *(Jm 2:19)*

Genuine faith must involve love of God, and is measured by its effect on heart and mind. Faith will affect thoughts, words and deeds. It will shape the soul for heaven. Conduct is clear evidence of that effect. A mindless repetition of dogma, or hate cloaked in fanaticism, is not the faith that leads to salvation. Indeed, such approaches evidence the rejection, not the acceptance, of the fundamental truths of faith. A very clear warning is given on this:

"Anyone who says 'I love God' and hates his brother, is a liar; since no one who fails to love his brother whom he can see can love God whom he has not seen." (*1 Jn* 4:20).

There are clear warnings on the difference between process and product, for those who consider themselves practising Christians. What matters is the effect on our heart and mind, not any outward statement or conformity.

Have we persisted in seeking the priority of our will, or have we sought to know God's will, and do that?

It is not anyone who says to me "Lord, Lord" who will enter heaven, but the person who does the will of my Father in heaven. When the day comes, many will say to me, "Lord, Lord, did we not prophesy in your name, drive out demons in your name, work many miracles in your name?" Then I shall tell them to their faces: I have never known you; away from me, all evil doers. (*Mt* 7:21-23)

What fate for the faithless?

The importance of faith raises difficult questions about the position of those apparently without it.

What of a person living in a culture, in a society or a family, ignorant, dismissive or derisive of the tenets of

Christian faith? Such a person may, of course, come to hear and love Jesus; but most in those circumstances will not. They will never attain specific knowledge of, and assent to, Christian faith.

What of the case of the person, perhaps showing real charity to others, who simply cannot find it in heart and mind to believe? We all know of examples from personal experience.

What of the person who once had a deep faith, but suddenly experiences doubt and emptiness? The conviction previously ever present, almost taken for granted, is absent. Attempts to reach God, to hear or see, come to naught; the dark night of the soul has come. This is a hard predicament. The individual knows well what appears to be lost, and fears the consequences. But effort alone is, for the time being, unavailing.

What of the individual crushed in spirit by illness or misfortune? Some, noble souls indeed, may be elevated, refined by suffering. But many are, we fear, ground down, sad and embittered. What is their fate?

We simply do not know. Clearly, the safe route is a life lived in faith, and in accordance with faith.

For those others, who cannot in this bodily life reach the haven of an express faith, may they somehow come safely ashore?

It appears to be in accordance with God's character and purpose that they will. It is worth noting that the quotation from John (3:36) refers to "refusal" to believe. That must mean a deliberate choice, based on knowledge, freedom and adequate means to reach that choice.

Many of those in the examples above will not have a genuine freedom to choose. They will not have "refused", in the sense of having made a free and informed choice. There is hope for them.

The suggestion of a decision at the moment of death, made by the soul in the shape in which it exists after all the acts and decisions of life have shaped it, accords with this wider view.

The shape created by a whole life is not lost by the mental anguish of a final illness, does not depend on knowledge or technical professions but on the soul's essential character: does it wish to leave all else, and come to God? When, at the last, the soul sees God and is invited to heaven, does it have the love and trust to say "Yes"?

8.3 Works

Then the upright will say to him in reply, "Lord, when did we see you hungry and feed you, or thirsty and give you drink ?"... And the king will answer, "In truth I tell you, in so far as you did this to one of the least of these brothers of mine, you did it to me."

(*Mt* 25:37-40)

How does it help, my brothers, when someone who has never done a single good act claims to have faith? Will that faith bring salvation ? If one of the brothers or one of the sisters is in need of clothes and has not enough food to live on, and one of you says to them, "I wish you well; keep yourself warm and eat plenty", without giving them these bare necessities of life, then what good is that? In the same way faith: if good deeds do not go with it, it is quite dead.

(*Jm* 2:14-17)

And that which is dead, decays. In a sense, all this is obvious. We can readily understand the accusation of hypocrisy levelled at the man who claims to be a Christian, attends services, has theological knowledge, but declines to help the poor. He has failed in the injunction to love his neighbour - one of the two greatest commandments: to love God and your neighbour (*Mt* 12:28-31).

So far, so good. We need to perform good works because it is one of the two great commandments, and to keep our faith alive.

Is there a measure? How many good deeds, and how onerous? Do we need simply to do more good deeds than bad? Or good deeds of a weight or seriousness greater than our bad deeds? Or does it depend on our capacity - are we required to do at least 75% (for example) by number and weight of what we could have done?

A common concern - but a misconceived one, and as absurd as to ask if an hour is yellow.

We do not face an exam, with a pass mark.

We do face a decision, and one made by our soul in its state at the moment of death.

We have a continuing obligation to do good. The specific occasions and opportunities will depend on our circumstances. We are warned that those with much (of whatever kind - wealth, power, intellect, strength, personality, talent) will face high demands - much will be expected of them (*Lk* 12:48).

The better, more serious, response to the banker with a large bonus should not be anger or contempt, or jealous plans or approval for confiscation (which all harm the onlooker), but a reminder and a warning: you are placed in a position to do much good. Make proper use of that power, for your own soul's sake.

All our acts, thoughts, words, will shape our soul. As we think along particular lines, we apparently establish or reinforce our neural canals; that facilitates further thought along the same lines. The mind we form directs our future thoughts and words and deeds.

Every unselfish (or selfish) act begets another of the same kind. We form our character by repetition. Each time we decline to seek out such an opportunity to help, each time we pass by on the other side of the road, we add to the weight of our soul on the side leaning away from heaven. We make it a little harder for that soul to have the character that will accept the invitation to sell all else, and buy the pearl beyond price: heaven.

9. On Death

Death is a man's first completely personal act, and is, therefore, by reason of its very being, the place above all others for the awakening of consciousness, for freedom, for the encounter with God, for the final decision about his eternal destiny.

The Moment of Truth: Fr Ladislaus Boros SJ

I am not dying; I am entering into life.

St Thérèse of Lisieux (1873-1897
[Words spoken shortly before death]

9.1 The moment of death

Some of us have seen human death. Many doctors and nurses, and clergy will have done so. Those in the armed forces and emergency services may have done so. Some of us will have been present at the death of a family member.

Sadly, this is an area where common knowledge and understanding has declined in the last 50 years. Far fewer people are now present at family deaths. The store of shared experience, the recollection of edifying tales of the passing of relations and friends, is depleted, scarcely existent. We lose much, in education and preparation, as a result.

If we have not seen the moment of death, we have probably seen someone not far from death - perhaps when visiting a family member in hospital. We can imagine, at least to some extent, how it feels to realize that one's own death is close.

There is, of course, a great gulf between observing the approach to death (or even death itself) of another, and experiencing it ourselves.

What the observer sees is clinical death: the cessation of essential bodily functions, with no revival. Defining this moment becomes more complex with advances in medical science. Clinically dead patients may be revived, with the injection of drugs, supply of oxygen, heart massage and other treatment. Indeed, even after irrevocable death, organs may be kept functioning, and even successfully transplanted.

There is, however, a fundamental point: to recognize the distinction between the physical and the spiritual - the fate of the body and the fate of the soul.

From the perspective of heaven, from the interest of the deceased, the important event is the spiritual consequence of death. This is the freeing of soul from body. For the first time the soul casts off from the material, from time, from space, from the demands of mind and body.

9.2 The soul alone

In death the spiritual movement of being is liberated from the alien element of non-personal temporality. The spirit's succession now becomes entirely interior, by the succession inherent in its exercise of its own being. This occurs in a total awareness and presence of being, and not in mere flashes that reach us only fragmentarily. Thus the spirit is no longer swept along by an alien succession. It is able to realize fully the whole continuity of its being, all at once, in one and the same act.

The Moment of Truth: Fr Ladislaus Boros SJ

At the moment of death, the soul can for the first time be entirely, and only, itself. This concept is wholly foreign to our daily experience. We are completely and only used to an intermediation - of mind, will, body - between the essential "me" and what we think or say or do.

One consequence is that the soul will be, will be seen, and will respond, exactly as it is. It will be in a state of, and express only, the complete truth about itself.

This is a sobering concept. We are so used to a degree of calculation, presentation, even dissimulation in our lives. From the social courtesies which make daily life easier, to the marketing essential for commercial work, or the courtier-like behaviour with superiors or others we wish to persuade or impress, we are used to a shading (at least) of the truth. We rarely speak or act precisely - no more, no less - as we think, see, feel or understand. On earth, we may even find it hard to discern the truth about ourselves. We are pressed by the material, by our culture, by our health and emotion, by our tendency to excuse or mitigate, perhaps even by a degree of mental anxiety or even despair.

Ourself, in truth alone, before God

Our familiarity with a process involving thought and calculation, our actions being determined thereby, is so engrained in life that it can readily mislead us when thinking about heaven and hell. We can too easily imagine that, if indeed we find there is a God, we will (as we would on earth) tailor our response accordingly: perhaps apologise for our sins and want of belief; present the most credible excuses we can imagine; ask, flatteringly, for pardon; seek entry to heaven.

That is to import our powers and manners on earth, as it were at the moment before death, to the moment of our death itself. That is a different place, one difficult to analyse. It is the meeting place of the book and the bookend. It is a moment infused with each element, but neither wholly one or other, where time meets eternity.

At the moment of death we can no longer calculate or dissimulate. Our soul, shaped in life, speaks out, makes its choice for God and heaven, or against. Its response is an unqualified expression of its shape, its essential nature at that moment.

Our soul expresses what it is, asks exactly what its nature requires, says exactly what it truly wants.

10. Entry Into Heaven

I am standing at the door, knocking. If one of you hears me calling and opens the door, I will come in to share a meal at that person's side.

(Rv 3:20)

Ask, and it will be given to you; search, and you will find; knock, and the door will be opened to you. Everyone who asks, receives; everyone who searches, finds; everyone who knocks will have the door opened.

(Mt 7:7-8)

10.1 The most important issue

Do not be afraid of those who kill the body but cannot kill the soul; fear him rather who can destroy both body and soul in hell.

(Mt 10:28)

It becomes us to spend this life only as a journey toward heaven….to which we should subordinate all other concerns of life. Why should we labour for or set our hearts on everything else, but that which is our proper end, true happiness?

Jonathan Edwards (1703-1758):
quoted in *Heaven* by Randy Alcorn

If heaven exists, arriving there must be the most important goal each of us will ever have.

We may be limited in vision or understanding; mistaken in theology, poor, undistinguished, unfortunate, unsuccessful, ignorant, unattractive, weak physically or psychologically, lacking in skill or talent. None of that matters compared to finding our way into heaven.

This chapter considers how we may enter heaven.

10.2 The character, purpose and consistency of God

"…I, Yahweh, do not change."

(*Ml* 3:6)

Jesus Christ is the same today as he was yesterday and as he will be forever.

(*Heb* 13:8)

The Lord is not slow in carrying out his promises, as some people think he is; rather is he being patient with you, wanting nobody to be lost and everybody to be brought to repentance.

(*2 P* 3:9)

In reflecting on how we come to heaven, our understanding of the character, purpose and consistency of God is an overarching theme. Specific theories about judgement need to be tested against this fundamental. God does not act inconsistently with his character or purpose. He will not set a test or make a judgement in relation to our entry into heaven which does not accord with his nature or purpose, as revealed to us.

The fundamentals we know are that:

- God created mankind deliberately, so that we could find joy and fulfilment with God, in heaven (*Mt* 25:34);
- God gave each of us free will, to accept or reject his love (*Lk* 9: 23; *Jn* 6:40);
- Even when our nature became corrupted, God still loved us so much that the second person of the Trinity came to earth, to suffer terribly and die in order to open a gateway to heaven - and so to our eternal joy and fulfilment (*Jn* 3:15-17);
- God desires every human ever born to come to heaven (*Lk* 15:11-32, the Prodigal Son)
- Nothing evil may endure in the presence of God in heaven (*Is* 59:2; *Rv* 21:27; *1 Co* 6:9-16; *Ga* 5:19-22).

Those features are the key guides to understanding how we enter heaven.

10.3 Free will

Enter by the narrow gate, since the road that leads to destruction is wide and spacious, and many take it; but it is a narrow gate and a hard road that leads to life, and only a few find it.

(*Mt* 7:13-14)

Free will is an essential element of our relationship with God. It is at the heart of our understanding of how the world is constructed and how God acts towards it. Its fundamental, structural importance supports the speculation that it continues into the moment of death, and our final acceptance or rejection of God.

That is important. Its impact is that we are neither chosen nor rejected; we will choose. We will, as it were, be the jury in our own trial. We will give the verdict, choosing heaven or hell ourselves. Our choice will be the inevitable expression of the nature of our soul, as we have shaped it through life.

This moment-of-death choice is a genuine choice. Each of us will have freedom to choose heaven or hell. But the choice is made by our soul as we have formed it in life. Every grain of decision, experience, will, sacrifice, generosity - and selfishness - exercised and created in life goes to shape our soul at that moment. That all contributes to our choice. It would be foolish to assume that a soul shaped to selfishness by its choices in life could choose God, could elect to abandon self-will, at the moment of death.

The role of God is not that of examiner or selector. It is a role of revelation and power. In his light, we will see what we truly are, the destination we are truly fitted for. Perhaps God's role is somewhat analogous to that of a judge in a jury trial. He accepts the verdict (chosen by the jury - here the soul at the moment of death). He pronounces the sentence, formalising the effect of the soul's choice and providing the power to move the soul to its chosen place, heaven or hell. He is in charge, his power moves events forward; but that power respects the freedom of choice of the individual soul.

We make our choice. God recognises it, respects it and acts upon it.

10.4 Only one question

The kingdom of heaven may be compared to a king who gave a feast for his son's wedding. He sent his servants to call those who had been invited, but they would not come. Next he sent some more servants with the words, "Tell those who have been invited: look, my banquet is all prepared, my oxen and fatted cattle have been slaughtered, everything is ready. Come to the wedding." But they were not interested; one went off to his farm, another to his business, and the rest seized his servants, maltreated them and killed them.

(*Mt* 22:1-7)

What the fall was for the angels, that death is for man.

St John of Damascus (675/6-749)

There is only one question our soul will face: Will you accept God, and enter into heaven?

Indeed, it is rather an invitation than an exam. At the moment of death we are invited to come to God, and enter heaven; but we can refuse. There lies our peril.

Who would refuse? Surely no one in their right mind? Surely no one would be so mad, so determined to damage themselves?

The answer is that it appears some have or will. The reason lies in the condition attached to entry; the shape of our soul; the soul's appreciation of itself, its own true character; and the truthfulness of every soul's response.

10.5 Only one condition

The kingdom of heaven is like treasure hidden in a field which someone has found; he hides it again, goes off in his joy, sells everything he owns and buys the field. Again, the kingdom of heaven is like a merchant looking for fine pearls; when he finds one of great value he goes and sells everything he owns and buys it.

(Mt 13:44-45)

Anyone who wants to save his life will lose it; but anyone who loses his life for my sake will find it. What, then, will anyone gain by winning the whole world and forfeiting his life ? Or what can anyone offer in exchange for his life ?

(Mt 16:25-26)

Only God is necessary. He is everything. The rest is nothing. All the rest vanishes before his face, and all the nations are as nothing in his sight. He is the one thing necessary to man. It is he alone whom we must desire, and to him alone that we must be united.

Letter to Madame d'Albert de Lyunes, 1695: Jacques-Bénigne Bossuet, Bishop of Meaux (1627-1704)

These two parables - the treasure hidden in the field and the merchant and the pearl - are particularly vivid and insightful. They explain the choice we are offered, and the only terms or conditions on which we can come to heaven.

The price of heaven is everything else. The treasure finder and the merchant did not use only part of their assets. They had to sell everything - stock, assets, home, personal possessions. Only in that way - and in no other- could the price of heaven be paid.

What will we have to sell?

The answer is, all the parts of our selves inconsistent with heaven - and we must do so willingly.

All our elements of "me first"; "I know better". All our relentless will to have our way; to have control; the habit of command; the desire to possess. All our pride in ourselves, our superior wit or strength or skill or possessions or reputation or place or appearance. And the renunciation goes further - to our hatreds, bitterness, contempt. All must be cast away. We must come to an unqualified acceptance of our essential selves, past (our life); present (our death) and future (in heaven); no regrets, no ambitions, no pride - only love of God and, by that, acceptance of all that was, is and will be.

In summary, we must renounce our pride, admit our need and yield our will to God. This is the narrow path we must tread.

We are left with our essential selves, as we were always intended to be, free of sin and the inclination to sin.

It will be as for the moving and strengthening words of Mr Valiant-for-Truth:

"I am going to my Father's. Though with great difficulty I reached here, I do not regret the troubles I have had. My sword I give to him that succeeds me in my pilgrimage. My courage and skill I leave to him that can get it. My marks and scars I carry with me as a witness that I have fought the battles of him who will now be my reward."

The Pilgrim's Progress: John Bunyan (1628-1688)

10.6 Who would choose Hell?

Jesus looked at him and said, "How hard it is for those who have riches to make their way into the kingdom of God ! Yes, it is easier for a camel to pass through the eye of a needle than for someone rich to enter the kingdom of God." Those who were listening said, "In that case, who can be saved?" He replied, "Things that are impossible by human resources, are possible for God".

(*Lk* 18:24–27)

The rich man faces a hard road indeed.

His life is likely to have offered a habit of command, an expectation of control, a persistent ability to make his own choice and carry it through. He will have made many decisions affecting others. He will have had many opportunities to help his neighbour. He will have found all too many occasions on which to decide against charity, to prefer self, seek the glitter of possessions, the enjoyment of self-will in power, the pride of comparison. His position, his world, his social connections, will all tend - like a tide or a slope - to carry him away from unselfishness and charity. That decline is not inevitable; but it is a real danger, a current to swim against.

The review of the rich man's life will be a full one. There will be much for him to understand. He will face the immense power and love of God; be bathed in extraordinary light.

What is the true response of this soul? Is it conviction of its sin and error; deep, painful contrition; repentance; a desperate plea for help? Indeed, is it so genuine, deeply felt and agonized as to be pared down to its essence: a simple cry: "Lord, help me?"

This is his (and, in due time, our) fundamental choice; it is worth our deep reflection now. Of course, a top of the head response may be that, faced with the presence and reality of God, the prospect of heaven or hell, obviously he (and we) will choose heaven. But is it so simple?

How do our own hearts work?

How easy do we find to give up self, at all - let alone entirely; to give up our will, our choice, our preference? How easy do we find it to trust another, at all - let alone completely?

We have to remember that the choice is an absolute one - to give up all else for heaven. We cannot retain the smallest part of our selfishness. To insist on retaining any is to choose against heaven. And we have to remember that there is no flannel, no deception, no mental reservation in our answer. Our soul will speak exactly as it is, express, entirely honestly, its nature.

We will have a choice something akin to that of the angels, or of Adam. We can choose to be with God; or we can seek to be "little gods" - maintaining our self, "without God, before God and not in accordance with God."

St Maximus the Confessor (580-662).

The terrible danger is that a soul shaped in life by selfishness can no longer come to God, voluntarily making a choice that it knows must mean the destruction, the burning away, of all that is inconsistent. The soul does indeed find the treasure in the field, recognise the pearl beyond price, understands its value - but cannot bring itself to part with all else in order to buy it.

This may sound strange, but reflection on our inner selves brings pause. Day by day, by every thought, word and deed, we could be moving towards God. We could be giving up (or at least reducing) our desire to put self first. Are we?

Or are we in effect saying that we will give up all these worldly things only when we have to - when death tears us away? But, of course, that is "giving up" nothing; we have already parted from the material world. The reality of our choice in that case is an absolute refusal to renounce anything up to (and including) the very last instant at which we had a choice.

What would that do to us? We would remain governed by our appetite to the very end. Indeed it is hard to see that we would have any true self left. We would be nothing apart from those dominating appetites which ruled us - for if we have something we cannot give up, we no longer own it; we are its slaves - it owns us.

The risk is that, at the end, we choose to retain selfishness over self; pride over love. We say, my will shall prevail; I will keep what I want; I will not trust God. Though in death my power is proved less than God's, I will not yield. I will not accept God as he is, and his sovereignty as it is.

Milton's terrible, magnificently conveyed choice of Satan is made again. It is lesser, of course, but the sinner's soul follows its Satanic master:

All is not lost; the unconquerable will,
And study of revenge, immortal hate,
And courage never to submit or yield:
And what is else not to be overcome ?
That glory never shall His wrath or might
Extort from me, to bow and sue for grace.

Paradise Lost: John Milton (1608-1674)

11. Purgatory

But we are not blissfully saved in having of our endless joy till we be all in peace and in love, that is to say, full pleased with God and with all his works. And with all his judgements, and loving and peaceable with our self, and with our even - Christian and with all whom God loves as love.

Shewings of Divine Love: Chapter 49:
Julian of Norwich (c. 1349-1416)

11.1 Authority and fundamentals

All who die in God's grace and friendship, but still imperfectly purified, are indeed assured of their eternal salvation, but after death they undergo purification, so as to achieve the holiness necessary to enter the joy of Heaven.

Catechism of the Catholic Church, para 1030

The idea of purgatory is prompted by: statements in the Bible; deduction from the revealed nature and purpose of God; traditional teaching of the Church; and a widely held, innate instinct. The Bible statements which prompt the idea of purgatory speak of proving or testing, they refer to fire (*1 Co* 3:15; *1 P* 1:7); they imply a forgiveness of sins after death (*Mt* 12:32). In the Old Testament there is reference to expiatory sacrifice made to assist the dead in coming to Heaven (*2 M* 12:46).

The deduction from Revelation is this:

- There is no place for sin with God in heaven.

- Even when we assent to God at the moment of death, our souls are in the shape we created in life. For most of us, our soul will bear the marks of sin, and retain an inclination to sin.

- In order to experience the full joy of heaven, we must cast away those marks, that attachment.

- We can only do so when we will it; when we have a full understanding of what we are doing; and with help.

The teaching of the Church in this area is long established. The doctrine was formulated particularly at the Councils of Florence (1439) and Trent (1563). It is closely connected with the practice, established in the very early church (noted by Tertullian, 160-220), of prayer for departed souls. Such a practice implies a process of purgatory in which departed souls can be assisted - since prayer cannot help those in hell, and is not needed by those in heaven.

Many of us hold a deeply felt conviction that the effect of our sins, our misshapen soul, should somehow be corrected, cleansed, balanced in ourselves, before we can enjoy the complete peace of heaven. C.S. Lewis expresses it well:

Our souls demand purgatory, don't they? Would it not break our heart if God said to us, "It is true my son that your breath smells and your rags drip with mud and slime, but we are charitable here and no one will upbraid you with these things, enter into joy"? Should we not reply, "With submission , Sir, and if there is no objection, I'd rather be cleaned first". "It may hurt, you know". "Even so, Sir".

Letters to Malcolm

A part of the assent to God

Purgatory is sometimes seen as a stage in our journey to heaven, part of a sequence. We die; we receive our particular judgement; we are purged; we enter into the full joy of heaven. This may be not far from the truth, but it risks misleading by introducing a worldly chronology into the picture.

It may be rather more helpful to see purgatory as part of our very assent to God, part of our acceptance of the invitation to heaven.

That assent and acceptance involves (as must every genuine "Yes") our understanding and will. We must fully understand our choice, including what must be left behind in order to enter heaven, and we must agree to that.

What we must leave behind is everything "unheavenly" in us.

The process of purgatory helps us both understand what must be left behind, and (given, and only if, we have chosen heaven, assented to God) helps us in the process of that casting away. It is the fire which burns away the "unheavenly" still in us. Of course, the more we have ourselves already cast away the unheavenly in our bodily life, the less extensive the purgatorial process.

11.2 Full truth

Yahweh, you examine me and know me,
You know when I sit, when I rise,
You understand my thoughts from afar,
You watch when I walk or lie down,
You know every detail of my conduct.

(Ps 139:1-3)

For there is nothing hidden, but it must be disclosed, nothing kept secret except to be brought to light.

(Mk 4:22)

Everything now covered up will be uncovered, and everything now hidden will be made clear. For this reason, whatever you have said in the dark will be heard in the daylight, and what you have whispered in hidden places will be proclaimed from the housetops.

(Lk 12:2-3)

In order to will to leave behind all unheavenly things in order to enter heaven, we must comprehend that "all".

Comprehension can only follow upon revelation and guidance. We will need to come to an understanding of the causes and consequences of our thoughts, words and deeds; how others were made to feel, encouraged to act, made to think, by our choices.

Some of our choices, long forgotten by us, will prove to have been unexpectedly good. The small help or advice or encouragement, which proved a turning point in the life of another. That almost careless gift to charity, made as we left the office for our Christmas break, which gave hope to a family in despair. Perhaps our only advocates, in this revealing, will be those we helped; the only voices speaking for us those to whom we gave with no thought of our own benefit.

Some other of our choices will prove unexpectedly, painfully, bad. Things we have forgotten, things we have excused, will be examined completely and justly. They will be revealed for exactly what they were. The thoughtless comment, the easy contempt, the denial or criticism which prompted another to despair. Our small selfishness which started or completed, hastened or encouraged, the pain, even ruin, of another.

Much, perhaps most, we will never have fully known, never have fully understood. Now we will do so. There is no hurry, no need for gloss or précis; no tact or flattery, no smiling courtesy avoiding the full, unvarnished truth. There is no place for excuse or justification, deceit or flannel or tosh. Just the full truth.

This revelation is not only directed to our assent in the sense of casting away what cannot be brought into heaven. It is also an essential part of the operation of our forgiveness. We come to understand the depth and nature of the forgiveness we need, and which we receive. It provokes an overwhelming gratitude and a complete peace.

We understand that all our sins are forgiven; nothing can be raised later. We will understand the immeasurable love of God.

11.3 A purging fire

For those who find themselves in a condition of being open to God but still imperfectly, the journey towards full beatitude requires a purification, which the faith of the Church illustrates in the doctrine of "purgatory".

General Audience, 4.8.1999:
John Paul II (1920-2005)

Does not the real Christianising of the early Jewish notion of a purging fire lie precisely in the insight that the purification involved does not happen through some thing but through the transforming power of the Lord himself, whose burning flame cuts free our closed off heart, melting it, and pouring it into a new mould to make it fit for the living organism of his body?"

Eschatology, p. 229: Cardinal Ratzinger
(later Pope Benedict XVI)

At the moment of our choice, before God, we will see ourselves exactly as we are. There will be no memory lapses, or polished tales. Absolute reality.

What an intense pain this process will involve for most of us.

To see how God has helped us, has always loved us, has provided every opportunity for us to develop and become our true selves. To understand what our true selves could have been. And to see how our determination not to listen, to follow our will, our selfish dreams, desires, pleasures, has meant we have missed opportunity after opportunity for ourselves, and have caused countless pains and miseries to others.

This is not a programme which can be switched off, a film we can leave, or a bad dream we can awaken from. This is the one, fundamental statement about our real selves. And we cannot deny or change it.

Reflecting on this, one can well understand why the analogy of consuming fire may be used for this coming to full understanding, and paring away of the unheavenly. Cardinal Ratzinger (later Pope Benedict XVI) described a purgatorial process in these terms:

"What actually saves is the full assent of faith. But in most of us, that basic option is buried under a great deal of wood, hay and straw. Only with difficulty can it peer out from behind the latticework of an egoism we are powerless to pull down with our own hands. Man is the recipient of the divine mercy, yet this does not exonerate him from the need to be transformed. Encounter with the Lord is this transformation. It is the fire that burns away our dross and re-forms us to be vessels of eternal joy."

(Eschatology, p 231)

We can readily understand this need for a process by which those elements in our soul which are unfit for heaven, for the presence of God, are removed. We can readily understand that the process involves some form of pain. And we can readily understand that it occurs only with our assent. Our soul has chosen God, and heaven. By doing so, it has recognised the need to remove those unfit parts, every attachment to evil. It consents, but it needs help to be cleansed, to cast away what is incompatible with heaven. It welcomes the process.

11.4 Time and triangles

Let us help and commemorate them. If Job's sons were purified by their father's sacrifice, why should we doubt that our offerings for the dead bring them some consolation? Let us not hesitate to help those who have died and offer our prayers for them.

St John Chrysostom (AD 347-407)

Heaven (and hell) are outside chronological time. This is, to us, a strange condition. We try to understand it by metaphor and picture. We need to approach these with caution. They are useful, but they have their limits. It is always a case of explaining sun by reference to snow (as it were); it is not exact, and poetry may convey a better meaning than prose.

One of our problems is a tendency to import worldly time - or at least a linear time concept - into heaven and hell, and their relationship with the world.

We naturally see history as a horizontal line, our own lives occupying a small section of that line. The line continues before and behind us. I look "back" to my ancestor Richard, who lived in the Midlands before the Reformation and is recorded as paying Hearth Tax. I see his life, as it were, some considerable way towards the left of the horizontal line marking the passage of history. I see myself much further "along", forward, towards the right.

How can I pray for Richard, when he was dead centuries before I was born? If we understand God as 'above' the line of worldly time, unlimited by place and size, then the line from Richard to God is no longer than the line from me to God.

Accordingly, while in worldly terms my prayer for my ancestor is made long after he is dead, for God that prayer is not "after" Richard's life. To God, Richard's prayers for his descendants, and mine for him, are not separated by (our) time. They both run up to God with no time gap. The length of those 'sides of the triangle' is equal. The prayers arrive "together". My prayer may in fact strengthen Richard against sin in his life in the early 16th century, so making his experience of the full truth of his life, in purgatory, somewhat easier. Who knows? In whatever way it may operate, prayer helps.

12. Vikings, Infants, the Insane and the Confused

[...God] wants everyone to be saved and reach full knowledge of the truth. For there is only one God, and there is only one mediator between God and humanity, himself a human being, Christ Jesus, who offered himself as a ransom for all.

(1 Tm 2:4-6)

For the ones that God will justify are not those who have heard the Law but those who have kept the Law. So, when gentiles, not having the Law, still through their own innate sense behave as the Law commands, then, even though they have no Law, they are a Law for themselves.

(Rm 2:13-14)

12.1 The desire to save the unknowing

Those who, through no fault of their own, do not know the gospel of Christ or his Church, but who nevertheless seek God with a sincere heart, and, moved by grace, try in their actions to do his will as they know it through the dictates of their conscience - those may achieve eternal salvation.

Lumen Gentium, 16 (1964)

A problem: if God does indeed wish that all mankind is saved, why is the only route through Jesus? Surely many people will never have heard of Jesus; are they disqualified from the outset? That looks hardly fair, hardly consistent with a plan for universal salvation.

The answer is to understand the role of Jesus. He makes our salvation possible notwithstanding that we are all inclined to sin, and will do so; and that heaven cannot include sin. But you can walk through a door without knowing it is there. If a gateway were ten (or a hundred) miles wide, many would. Nevertheless, their entry is unquestionably, and without exception, through that gateway.

God does indeed wish that we enter heaven. He invites us; his grace prompts us; the Holy Spirit informs us; but he gives us a free choice. It is up to us to assent. We are free to enter heaven, and free to decline.

Indeed, God does more. By the operation of his grace, a free and undeserved gift from God to every human, God assists us to respond affirmatively to his invitation. Grace operates, as it were, as flakes of metal infused into our soul prompting it to turn towards the magnetism of God. A limited analogy, of course; but intended to indicate the gift and its effect.

Difficult cases

The same choice is open to all. The fact that you never knew of Jesus, or followed another faith, does not remove your choice at the moment of death, or the possibility of reaching heaven. The viking, or any follower of another faith (or of none), may have made unselfish choices throughout their life. Such a soul may be well able to leave all else behind and choose God and heaven at the moment of death. All have the benefit of guidance by the Holy Spirit - even the child in the womb (*Lk* 1:15 - "even from his mother's womb he [John the Baptist] will be filled with the Holy Spirit").

The aborted foetus, the infant and the insane can make the same choice. Surely they will have a clear sight, in that moment of death? They are not called upon to rely on brain-power, knowledge or experience, in that instant when the temporal life is left behind and eternity begins. The confusion of a damaged brain, or a chemically induced cycle of despair, or a lack of mental development or experience and knowledge, are all elements of this material world. The choice for God and heaven does not depend on things, abilities, knowledge. The soul is faced with the bright light and power of God, and is simply invited to say yes, to come to heaven and be with God.

Why should we assume these souls are incapable of making a decision for God?

One can readily envisage that their limitations in worldly terms cease (or become irrelevant) in that moment of death, replaced with the ability to make a direct answer from the soul.

For the first time, the soul will see all clearly; will respond with the unencumbered totality of its being.

For these, what a strong likelihood of salvation. No selfishness, no years of self-preference, to cloud the choice.

13. The Safe Route

That neither skill nor knowledge is required to enable us to go to God, but just a heart determined to turn to Him only, to beat for him only, and to love him only.

The Practice of the Presence of God, The Third Conversation, 22nd November, 1666: Brother Lawrence to the Abbé de Beaufort.

And my ending is despair,
Unless I be relieved by prayer;
Which pierces so, that it assaults
Mercy itself, and frees all faults.
As you from crimes would pardoned be,
Let your indulgence set me free.

Epilogue, *The Tempest*:
William Shakespeare (1564-1616)

13.1 What is in your heart?

If anyone wants to be a follower of mine, let him renounce himself and take up his cross every day and follow me. Anyone who wants to save his life will lose it; but anyone who loses his life for my sake, will save it.

(Lk 9:23-24)

You are enslaved by the verb "to have"... The very mainspring of your activity is a demand, either for a continued possession of that which you have, or for something which as yet you have not: wealth, honour, success, social position, love, friendship, comfort, advancement.... These dispositions, so ordinary that they almost pass unnoticed, were named by our blunt forefathers the Seven Deadly Sins of Pride, Anger, Envy, Avarice, Sloth, Gluttony, and Lust.

Practical Mysticism: Evelyn Underhill (1875-1941)

Not everything we expect, or fear, occurs. Often, the path of history - personal, organisational, national - is determined by the unknown or the little regarded. No doubt we will meet in heaven many we did not expect and, perhaps, search in vain for many we did. Who can be sure of the shape of a man's soul at death?

Who can know what may have caused just enough change that the soul can answer "Yes" at that crucial point, can decide for heaven at the moment of death?

We have been warned, and encouraged, very clearly. We have been given clear guidance on the route to heaven. There is no need to play, or point in playing, hopscotch on the motorway. We have been shown a safe route.

Brother Lawrence sets out the basic principle. Every thought, and word and deed of ours should be guided by that principle. Of course we will fall short. Brother

Lawrence, the wounded ex-soldier, sometime footman, worker in the monastic kitchen, knew the remedy:

That when he was at fault he simply admitted it and said to God "I shall never do otherwise if you leave me to myself; it is for you to prevent my falling and to correct what is wrong". He then felt assured of God's forgiveness, and did not let the failing prey on his mind.

(*Second Conversation*, 28th September, 1666).

In other words, we need to be aware of our sins, and we need to repent. As in so many other areas, that is not a matter of form, process or words. It is a matter of the heart.

Repentance

Have we reached the place of genuine contrition? Have we come to the conviction that, if offered the choice of that sin again, we would wish to turn away from it? Repentance is not achieved by saying sorry. There must be a genuine turning away from the offence, a rejection of any remaining affection for that sin.

But if we do genuinely repent, what bliss! The sin is removed "as the distance of east from west, so far from us does he put our faults" (*Ps* 103:12)

We will sin; and if we do not repent, there lies our danger. All sin leads to suffering (for us and for others). But if, by the moment of our death, we have shaped our soul into such a form that it cannot accept the invitation to enter heaven - because it cannot cast away the priority of self - then our fate is terrible. We remain free to make our choice, to go our own way. Our path then leads to the only destination outside heaven - hell.

There is, of course, much more, and much more detailed guidance to meet specific needs. It lies in the Bible, interpreted in Church teaching, explained in the writings of theologians, illuminated in the words of mystics.

The Commandments

The Ten Commandments remain the framework (*Mt* 19:16), with Jesus's important gloss on priority:

Master, which is the greatest commandment of the law? Jesus said to him, You must love the Lord your God with all your heart with all your soul, and with all your mind. This is the greatest and the first commandment. The second resembles it: You must love your neighbour as yourself. On these two commandments hang the whole Law, and the prophets too.

(*Mt* 22:36-40)

Jesus has given us specific teaching on certain points. The advice implements the fundamental requirements to love God and neighbour.

Love: "Now love is nothing other than the firm constant willingness and desire and purpose to please God, and to conform our own wishes entirely to what he commands, rooting out from our hearts all that might displease him, even though it should cost us our lives." Jacques-Bénigne Bossuet, Bishop of Meaux (1627-1704)

Forgiveness: We must forgive others if we are to be forgiven (*Lk* 11:4; *Mt* 18:18, 23-35).

Humility: We must have humility - the reciprocal of the sin of pride. We must become like children (*Lk* 18:15-17); that is, we must be prepared to trust in God, not ourselves. We must give up our desire to control, to determine, to decide - all examples of our innate tendency to give priority to self.

Charity: We must evidence our love of neighbour in practical ways. That duty of practical help trumps caution, rules, culture and process, as shown in the Good Samaritan parable.

Prayer: Prospero has it right. Prayer does indeed pierce. This is moving and interesting phraseology - with a potentially dangerous reference (for an Elizabethan playwright) to indulgences. An echo of his father's Catholicism? Or from missing years spent as a tutor to a Lancastrian recusant household? Or derived from speculative discourse late at night, returning up Bread Street from the tavern, speaking dazzlingly with Fletcher or Johnson or Middleton, and perhaps overheard by the child John Milton, looking out onto Bread Street from the windows of his father's house? Whatever the genesis, Shakespeare touches a nerve. Prayer is a fundamental link for us with God; with God's power, and for our understanding and preservation. We need it, by us and for us.

In the end, it all comes down to the state of our innermost being, our soul. That needs to be full of love. To the extent that it contains other preferences - for power, wealth, control, possessions, passions, there is no room for love.

If, in the end, we have shaped a soul that is weighted away from love, so that it cannot give up these other things, we will say "No" to heaven. We will choose hell.

Our choice will be respected.

14. Doubt and Encouragement

"...lately I find myself constantly attacked by thoughts. God knows if sins can really be prayed away. And it is a hard life, you know. And then, is it really true what that book says - that dead men will be resurrected?....For that matter, who really knows if there will even be a hell - right?.....Maybe that book was written by some clergy, by some high authorities, just to scare us fools to make us more humble. Life is full of hardships as it is, without any consolation - and there won't be any in the next life. So what's the point?"

The Way of a Pilgrim: Anon, Russian, 1881

Go and find him when your strength and patience are giving out, when you feel lonely and helpless. Say to him: "You know well what is happening, my dear Jesus. I have only you. Come to my aid." And then go your way, and don't worry about how you are going to manage. It is enough to have told our good Lord. He has an excellent memory.

St Jeanne Jugan (1792-1879)

14.1 On war

Keep sober and alert, because your enemy the devil is on the prowl like a roaring lion, looking for someone to devour. Stand up to him, strong in faith and in the knowledge that it is the same kind of suffering that the community of your brothers throughout the world is undergoing.

(1 P 5:8)

Tell the men not to lose heart. Fight on.

Last words of Lt Col W. Elstob VC, DSO, MC,
Manchester Hill, St Quentin, 21st March 1918

Within, we should seek and may from time to time (even much of the time) find, the peace of God. But outside, we are at war. The fact of war does not depend on us. We have no option to negotiate a compromise or offer concessions to appease. Our choice is stark: fight, or be destroyed.

That is not so strange. We have seen that case too often in the history of the world. Even where our enemy is man, prone to weakness, inconsistency, idleness, open to bribe and flattery - yet still, sometimes, we see the terrible choice - fight, or yield and be destroyed in terror.

In the spiritual realm, we face a far more formidable foe than any man. Our enemy is powerful, relentless, closed to pity or persuasion. If we chose, as it were, to walk about No Man's Land, whistling brightly and saying, "hello clouds, hello sky", we will get a bullet in the lungs or a bayonet in the guts. There are no deals to be done, no "live and let live".

We need to be aware of our enemy, and that we are at war. Satan's legions will attack us, seeking to replace love in our heart with alternatives purporting to offer comfort, convenience, pleasure. He will attack our faith, to remove the underlying certainty and trust directing our conduct. No one is immune.

Above all, our enemy will practice deception. We must expect that: when he lies, he speaks his natural language, for he is a liar and the father of lies (*Jn* 8:44).

The doubts of the poor forester, relayed to the pilgrim in Russia in the mid-19th century, and recorded in *The Way of a Pilgrim*, echo with us. Satan and his legions are a formidable enemy, and master of effective lies.

The starting point for resistance is to know you are at war.

14.2 God's nature and purpose

For the mountains may go away and the hills may totter, but my faithful love will never leave you, my covenant of peace will never totter, says Yahweh who takes pity on you.
(*Is* 54:10)

Looking into our own heart can be lowering. Even given our limited self-knowledge, our over-readiness to find excuses, it is still a grim prospect. We all know that we fall short. We do not do as we should, and could. Any honest judgement would find us worthy of punishment.

Realism is good, but defeatism is not. We should acknowledge our failings, but not despair. The reason lies in God's nature and his purpose for us.

God created us, deliberately, for a purpose. The purpose is for us to come to know and love God, and live in heaven with him. God is unchanging and omnipotent. He makes this possible.

Above all, God acts towards us out of complete and unchanging love. That love is not lost, is not withdrawn by reason of our sins and failings. It is always there for us, whenever we turn to it.

Our understanding of God's nature and purpose has developed over history. The Jewish people enjoyed clear, fundamental and cohesive insights. Even while still awaiting further enlightenment, they understood God's extraordinary love (*Ps* 57) and his role as creator (*Is* 40:12). This understanding came early. The Psalms were written by or at the direction of King David (1040 - 970 BC); and Isaiah made his prophesies between about 735BC and 700BC.

In the Christian era these thoughts are further developed. John writes:

My dear friends,
let us love each other,
since love is from God.

And everyone who loves is a child of God and knows God.
Whoever fails to love does not know God,
because God is love.
This is the revelation of God's love for us,
That God sent his only son into the world
That we might have life through him
Love consists in this:
It is not we who loved God,
But God loved us and sent his Son
To expiate our sins.

(1 Jn 4:7-10)

That is an abiding source of confidence. God desires our company. He wants us to make the right decision, to come to Heaven.

15. Summary

It is truly perfect love when anyone still mortal rejoices only in God, and wants nothing and desires nothing except God and for God's sake. And so we know that holiness does not consist in the crying out of the heart, or in tears, or in external works, but in the sweetness of perfect love and heavenly contemplation.

The Fire of Love: Richard Rolle (1300 - 1349): quoted in *The Way of the English Mystics:* Gordon L. Miller

15.1 God's love, our choice

Sell your possessions and give to those in need. Get yourselves purses that do not wear out, treasure that will not fail you, in heaven where no thief can reach it and no moth destroy it. For wherever your treasure is, that is where your heart will be too.

(Lk 12; 33-34)

For God sent his son into the world
Not to judge the world,
But so that through him the world might be saved.
No one who believes in him will be judged;
But whoever does not believe is judged already,
Because that person does not believe
In the Name of God's only Son.

And the judgement is this:
Though the light has come into the world
People have preferred darkness to the light
Because their deeds were evil.

(*Jn* 3:17-19)

God loves each and every one of us. Whatever our nation, talents, length of life, psychological state, background.

God desires each and every one of us to come to heaven.

God will not play games with us, not set tests we cannot pass or make judgements against us. He wishes us to choose him. He will forgive every sin for which we ask forgiveness, genuinely repenting.

God has given us free will, and will not override that. If we choose against him, that choice will be respected.

At the moment of death, we will be invited to come to God, to enter heaven. We may accept or reject that invitation.

Our decision is made by our soul - our essential, fundamental being. There is no room, in our response to God's invitation, for deceit or calculation or flattery. We will give a completely truthful answer. That answer depends on what our soul truly desires: to come to God, or not.

What our soul desires depends on its character. That is shaped throughout our life by our choices. While our soul will be far from spotless, it can nevertheless be inclined to

God - or not. It is entirely possible to shape our soul into a form which rejects the invitation to come to God.

Coming to heaven means coming to heaven as it is - a sinless place. We must leave behind all parts of our "me first" character, all desire for personal control, all our sinful inclination to selfishness. The pearl beyond price can only be purchased by giving up all - absolutely all - else.

We must also trust God. This trust flows from love, and is "childlike"; there is no reservation for our own power and control.

The encounter with God, and the knowledge of our absolute forgiveness, must involve an understanding on our part of the nature and scale of that forgiveness. That means an audit of our life, showing the nature of all our acts (and thoughts and words): all this in the brilliant light of Christ's love.

This is a process both joyful (for we are willing to cast away all our sin, and we experience the overwhelming love and forgiveness of God, and know we are to be with him eternally in heaven) and intensely painful. We will see those occasions where we preferred self and harmed others; where our selfish choice to please our will cost some others dear indeed. We will see the pain we caused, the opportunities missed, the help we received and for which we gave no thanks.

15.2 Heaven and Hell

Human beings are created to praise, reverence and serve God our Lord, and by means of this to save their souls. The other things on the face of the earth are created for the human beings, to help them in working toward the end for which they are created. From this it follows that I should use these things to the extent that they help me toward my end, and rid myself of them to the extent that they hinder me......I ought not to seek health rather than sickness, wealth rather than poverty, honour rather than dishonour, a long life rather than a short one, and so on in all other matters. I ought to desire and elect only the thing which is more conducive to the end for which I am created.

Spiritual Exercises: The First Week: Principle of Foundation: St Ignatius Loyola (1491-1556)

This, therefore, may serve as a touchstone, whereby everyone may try the truth of his state: if the old man is still a merchant within you, trading in all sorts of worldly honour, power or learning; if the wisdom of this world is not foolishness to you, if earthly interests and seasonal pleasures are still the desire of your heart, and only covered under a form of godliness, a cloak of creeds, observances and institutions of religion, you may be assured that the pearl of great price is not yet found by you.

William Law (1686-1761): quoted in *The Way of the English Mystics* by Gordon. L. Miller

We are able to experience a foretaste of heaven - albeit periodic and partial - in our life on earth. The closer we follow the injunction to love God and neighbour, the greater the experience .

After death, we come to the present heaven. We will have a direct relationship with God. We will be filled with joy. We will have companionship, be able to communicate and have some presence sufficient to identify ourselves and others. This heaven is, however, in a different dimension to our universe, and our powers should be understood by way of analogy, not necessarily as a direct replacement of our present powers.

At some future point, the Second Coming and Final Judgement will occur. We will then receive our resurrected bodies, and enjoy the new heaven, re-established on the new earth. The same complete joy and companionship with God will obtain, but now also the added fulfilment of our resurrected bodies and our additional roles in the new heaven.

Both present and future heaven will provide complete fulfilment and joy, far beyond anything we have experienced on earth. However, the terrible fact is that we have a choice. We can reject God's invitation, and go our own way. That way takes us, immediately and inevitably, to hell.

Hell is not a joke, not a reasonable alternative. It is terrible. Unending pain and despair, consciousness of our wilful rejection of God, our deliberate choice of utter misery.

Yet if offered the choice again and again, the soul in hell would always choose this same destination. It cannot give up self, whatever the cost.

15.3 Getting to Heaven

Two men went up to the Temple to pray, one a Pharisee, the other a tax collector. The Pharisee stood there and said this prayer to himself, "I thank you, God, that I am not grasping, unjust, adulterous like everyone else, and particularly that I am not like this tax collector here…" The tax collector stood some distance away, not daring even to raise his eyes to heaven; but he beat his breast and said, "God, be merciful to me, a sinner". This man, I tell you, went home justified; the other did not. For everyone who raises himself up will be humbled, but anyone who humbles himself will be raised up.

(*Lk* 18:10-14)

To love everything, everybody, always to sacrifice oneself for love, meant to love no one, meant not to live this earthly life. And the more imbued he was with the principle of love, the more he renounced life and the more completely he destroyed that dreadful barrier which, without love, stands between life and death.

War and Peace (the death of Prince Andrei):
Leo Tolstoy (1828-1910)

Getting to heaven is not complicated; it is a straight path. We have to shape our soul in life so that, at the moment of death, we can accept God's invitation to heaven.

That means being able to give up everything else, and being able to trust God.

The fundamental route for achieving a character which will make that choice is a practice of loving God and neighbour - the first creates trust in God, the second facilitates giving up all for God. Since we will, inevitably, fall short, we also need to repent genuinely of all our sins.

The Ten Commandments, and the words of the Bible, give us further guidance.

Shaping our soul for heaven will take decision and effort. Our final destination depends on this: what is the state of our soul? Where is our heart?

Deep, deep down: what do we truly love?

Bibliography

Alcorn, Randy, *Heaven* (Tyndale House, 2007)

Anon, *The Cloud of Unknowing*

Anon, *The Way of a Pilgrim*

Avila, St Teresa of, *Collected Works of St Teresa of Avila*

Benedict XVI, Pope (Josef Cardinal Ratzinger), *Eschatology: Death and Eternal Life* (Washington DC, Catholic University of America Press, 2007)

Boros, Ladislaus SJ *The Moment of Truth: Mysterium Mortis* (London, Burns & Oates, 1969)

Bossuet, Jacques- Bénigne, *Letters of Spiritual Direction*

Bunyan, John, *The Pilgrim's Progress*

Catechism of the Catholic Church

Churchill, Winston S., *Painting as a Pastime*

Coghill, Nevill, *Visions of Piers Plowman: taken from the Poem by William Langland*

Donne, John, *No Man Is An Island: A Selection from the Prose of John Donne* (ed. Rivers Scott; various editions)

Edwards, Jonathan, *The Christian Pilgrim*

Julian of Norwich, *Revelations of Divine Love*

Jung, Carl, *Memories, Dreams, Reflections*

Kahneman, Daniel, *Thinking, Fast and Slow* (London, Allen Lane, 2011)

Kempis, Thomas à, *The Imitation of Christ*

164

Kipling, Rudyard, *The Holy War*

Kubler-Ross, Elisabeth *On Life After Death* (2008)

Law, William, *The Spirit of Prayer and the Spirit of Love*

Lewis, C.S., *Letters to Malcolm: Chiefly on Prayer*; *Mere Christianity*

Loyola, St Ignatius, *Spiritual Exercises*

Miller, Gordon L., *The Way of the English Mystics*: *An Anthology and Guide for Pilgrims* (London, Continuum, 1996)

Milton, John, *Complete English Poems*

Pascal, Blaise, *Pensées*

Petrisko, Thomas W., *Inside Heaven and Hell*: *What History, Theology and the Mystics tell us about the Afterlife* (McKees Rocks PA, St Andrew's Productions, 2000)

Rules for the Conduct of Life for Freemen of London (various editions)

Shakespeare, William, *Complete Works*

Tolstoy, Leo, *War and Peace*

Trochu, François, *The Curé d' Ars*

Underhill, Evelyn, *Practical Mysticism*

Vatican II, *Dogmatic Constitution on the Church*: *Lumen Gentium*

Further Reading

Bryson, Bill, *A Short History of Nearly Everything* (London, Doubleday, 2003)

Cooper, Austin, Julian of Norwich: *Reflections on Selected Texts* (London, Continuum, 2001)

Damascus, St John of, *Fountain of Knowledge*

Holden, Anthony, *William Shakespeare* (London, Little, Brown, 1999)

Kreeft, Peter, *Everything You Ever Wanted To Know About Heaven but Never Dreamed of Asking* (San Francisco CA, Ignatius Press, 1990)

Lisieux, St Thérèse of, *Story of a Soul*

Robinson, Martin, *Sacred Places, Pilgrim Paths*: *An Anthology of Pilgrimage* (1997)

Schouppe, F.X. SJ, *Purgatory*: *Explained by the Lives and Legends of the Saints* (various editions)

Wilson, A.N., *A Life of John Milton* (Oxford, OUP, 1983)

Williams, Peter S., *The Case for God* (1999)

Acknowledgements

A number of people were kind enough to help me with their comments. I would like to thank in particular: Anthony Pugh Thomas, Richard Stones and Pauline Watford. Their contributions were enormously helpful and very much appreciated. However, the content of this booklet should not be taken to reflect their views. The Bible quotations in this booklet are taken from *The New Jerusalem Bible*.